Fundamental Filing Practice

OFFICE OCCUPATIONS SERIES

Al Giordano, Series Editor

FUNDAMENTAL FILING
PRACTICE

IRENE PLACE, Ed.D.
Professor, Portland State University, Oregon

ESTELLE L. POPHAM, Ph.D.
Professor Emeritus, Hunter College, New York

HARRY N. FUJITA
Records Officer, University of Washington, Seattle

Prentice-Hall, Inc., Englewood Cliffs, New Jersey

Library of Congress Cataloging in Publication Data

Place, Irene Magdaline (Glazik)
    Fundamental filing practice.

    (Office occupations series)
    Bibliography: p.
      1. Files and filing (Documents)   I. Popham, Estelle L., joint author.   II. Fujita,
Harry N., joint author.   III. Title.
HF5736.P62   651.5'3'076   74-39739
ISBN   0-13-332742-6

©1973 by Prentice-Hall, Inc.,
Englewood Cliffs, New Jersey

Printed in the United States of America

10   9   8   7   6   5   4   3   2

Prentice-Hall International, Inc., *London*
Prentice-Hall of Australia, Pty. Ltd., *Sydney*
Prentice-Hall of Canada, Ltd., *Toronto*
Prentice-Hall of India Private Limited, *New Delhi*
Prentice-Hall of Japan, Inc., *Tokyo*

Contents

Introduction

Memory is supported by written and graphic documents. One of the problems of our times is that we have tremendous stockpiles of documents. Every individual, every home, and every organization — large or small — has its own stockpile of written and graphic records. Such a stockpile is a potential asset to those who draw from it to refresh their memory. It supplies additional information, thus helping comprehension and thought processes. It supplies data which enhance rational processes, particularly the decision-making process. To have a stockpile of relevant records at hand is like having money in the bank, but it isn't any good unless you can take it out when you need it.

To be useful, a stockpile of relevant records must be *organized* so that any item can be found when it is needed. Therefore, records in big stockpiles, such as we find in business and government today, have to be classified, housed, managed, and systematized for quick retrieval — instant use. Unless this is done, the stockpile is of no value. Huge amounts of available information, the large number of people involved, the speed with which change is introduced, and the variety of machines and equipment we have to duplicate and to move data are some of the reasons why wise organization and management of records is essential in order to keep a company of any size or type healthy. To manage records so that they are a truly useful resource within such a complex of variables calls for carefully developed classifications and rational coordination of resources. It calls for organization and effective systems.

Since the 1950s, business and government records management specialists have given special attention to improving the control of files. Records management programs have been developed, and a body of practices and guidelines have resulted in creating classification, storage, and retrieval systems. Literature about business filing and records management has been written by such specialists as Bourne, Griffin, Kahn, Kallous, Leahy, Menkus, Odell, Shiff, Weeks, and Wylie (see Bibliography in Appendix).

This book translates into teachable projects ideas, practices, and systems developed by leading filing and records management practitioners. It also provides occupational guidance for students about an uncrowded occupational area in which interested, informed, and willing workers can progress rapidly.

Practical exercises throughout this book take students from the simple aspects of filing and records classification to the more sophisticated systems. They encompass the whole records-keeping spectrum. The exercises teach students how to work with alphabetic, numeric, geographic, subject, and functional filing systems for correspondence, unit record cards, tapes, and unconventional materials. They help them understand how to appraise filing systems, how to select and safeguard vital records, how to select equipment and supplies, and how to establish filing controls. They give them an understanding of records retention schedules and how to build them. Chapter content throughout the book provides information about retrieval systems, standards, equipment and supplies, coordinated systems, microfilming, mechanization, and record-keeping automation.

Undoubtedly, automation is changing information storage and retrieval systems. Hand filing is increasingly "horse-and-buggy." All filing, however, will not become automated tomorrow. Manual records manipulation is likely to continue into the foreseeable future as an important adjunct to automated record keeping. In this text we have, therefore, resisted a temptation to glamorize electronic data processing, computer output microfilm, and other new automatic innovations. Instead, we have tried to present practical fundamentals of good record keeping, starting with manual and mechanical systems so that the new computer applications can be understood in terms of basic practices and needs.

In researching the material for this book, we visited filing installations from simple ones used by an interior decorator and a realtor to a vast storage center deep in the caverns of the earth. We visited federal records centers, electronic data processing centers, the records center of a large hospital, and the archives of a huge industry. We attended national records conferences where mere educators were looked upon quizzically by records managers with vice-presidential status in information technology. We conferred with management consultants and specialists employed by filing equipment companies. We attended business shows where miles of record keeping equipment were displayed. From these experiences we developed teaching materials for *our* own classes, for this text, and — we hope — for *your* classes.

We acknowledge with sincere appreciation the assistance of many records managers and filing experts. We are grateful for the permission given us by many filing equipment suppliers to use their illustrations (see List of Suppliers in Appendix). Each illustration was carefully selected to teach, not merely to ornament the book.

Any teacher or student using this text will probably want to discuss filing and records management with local specialists, to visit filing installations, and to explore the extensive literature available (see Bibliography in Appendix). Students will want to secure catalogs and descriptive materials from equipment manufacturers listed in the Appendix. The Glossary (see Appendix) describes unfamiliar terms and clarifies familiar ones.

This book is designed primarily for the mature student: community college, university, business college, or special adult vocational program. In preparing the teaching-learning projects, which are such a large part of this text, the authors developed projects that involve decision making as well as knowledge about filing systems. Some attention is also given to the managerial aspects of record keeping. In our opinion, a records course at the college level is justified only if a student understands how to develop a comprehensive records management program based on sound management practices.

It is not likely that a teacher will have time to use all the projects given in this text. Some allowance can be made for individual differences, especially if students work through the text on an individual-contract, self-study basis. Some may want to dwell on filing and indexing exercises and projects relating primarily to beginning record-keeping jobs. Where a group goes through the text as a class, a teacher may want to by-pass some projects to allow more time for visits to local records centers, talks by records managers, and to discuss concepts which students develop from their readings and research. In other words, this text is flexible. It can be used as a simple, entry-level filing course or as the background of a community-oriented type course that helps students bridge the gap between the classroom and the real world. It can be used to prepare vocational office education students, particularly co-operative students, for a *career* in records management. It can also be used as a ready reference for filing projects in a simulated office course.

Irene Place

Estelle L. Popham

Harry N. Fujita

1

Fundamental Filing

An effective filing system is one of man's most valuable tools. It keeps his records in an orderly way so that he can find them when he wants them. Because man forgets easily, he must use filing systems of different kinds to store information which supplements his memory. Unless he does this, he wastes time looking for information he needs and gets frustrated and upset doing so — especially when he can't find it. If he is in business, he may go broke because he cannot find vital information. It is said that inadequate records pave the way to bankruptcy.

Fundamental Filing Problems

Because things change faster and faster as our civilization grows more mature, and because man forgets easily, information is a perishable commodity. It deteriorates and is forgotten unless it is recorded. It is very important for people to preserve information not only for use during their lifetimes but for following generations as well. Unless information gained from discoveries, inventions, and experiences of people is preserved, future generations will suffer because they will not have the information they need to learn about the past. Files are a means of preserving and accumulating knowledge. Files can become a reservoir of information from which many people, now and in the future, may learn.

The problem of preserving records that will supplement man's unreliable memory and help him use the results of past experiences is not a new one. It was a problem during the stone age. At that time, picture records were chiseled into rocks and painted on the walls of caves. Later, when man learned how to make paper and how to write and print, it became possible to store information on paper. For a while, paper records really did solve the problem of preserving information. Then, duplicating machines and automatic typewriters came along to produce hundreds of paper copies of records an hour. Today, therefore, we have a new filing problem — regular haystacks of records such as letters, invoices, order forms, government forms, punched cards, tapes, books, catalogs, personnel records, checks, and microfilm, to name a few. Today's filing includes, therefore, the added problem of deciding what records to throw away and how to keep useless extra copies and junk out of the files.

Before paperwork became a serious problem in business, the purpose of filing was primarily to store accumulations of records out of the way and into some safer place than in a desk. Business is still interested, of course, in safeguarding its records, but the new emphasis is on the coordination and fast retrieval of filed *information.* Information may be derived from an accumulation of organized records. That is, systematically organized accumulations of records are more likely to produce reliable information than those which are not systematically organized. Such systems need to be planned, controlled, protected, and maintained by competent personnel.

Controlling Files

The office is the nerve center of a business; office files are the memory. Office files have information on which decisions are based and actions taken that determine the success or failure of the business. Every business needs an effective office information system.

In business, information processing and record keeping are a major part of office work. Anyone, therefore, who expects to be an office worker must know something about developing and controlling good, workable information filing systems. Records can be effectively controlled only when they are organized, safely stored, and handled by trained people. The tons of records that move through a modern office are of little value unless the information they supply is readily available when needed. If a record cannot be found when needed, it might as well not have been made. It is a waste.

Organizing Files

Organizing files is a first step in controlling them. Organization is the opposite of confusion or mixup. To organize is to arrange items in some logical sequence. To be most useful, a filing system must be logical and must follow a meaningful pattern of organization. Files can be organized alphabetically by name, subject, geographic location, or numerically by date or number. These different types of filing systems are all described later in this Workbook. The point to understand here is that a first step in controlling files is to organize them according to meaningful, logical classifications so that they will not become haystacks of jumbled, mixed-up items.

Safeguarding Files

Records need to be protected from humidity, dirt, fire, loss, prying eyes, rough treatment, and the erosion of time. If they are not protected, they may be destroyed, deteriorate so that they are not useful, or be lost so they cannot be found when needed. Over the years, many types of filing cabinets, folders, and guides have been developed to help safeguard files. Procedures also have been developed for handling them carefully. Because safeguarding files is an important part of filing fundamentals, filing supplies and equipment are covered in Chapter 5 of this Workbook and filing practices are covered in Chapter 3.

Filing Personnel

Effective filing and retrieval systems need people who are interested in organizing records so that they can be found easily when wanted. They need people who care, who take pride in their work, and who know about different filing systems, equipment and supplies, and about up-to-date filing practices. Filing personnel should be well trained and dependable because, when a record is misplaced or incorrectly filed, it may not show up for months. This may mean the loss of business. It may also cause frustration, fault finding, and grief. Well-trained filing and record-keeping personnel can help to eliminate such problems.

Everyone, from a repairman, a delivery man, and a housewife, to an executive, a file clerk, a secretary, a data processing specialist, and a librarian, handles records and files. However, these different people need differing degrees of filing expertise. Knowing how to set up and maintain a filing system is more important for some than others. For example, classifying books and materials and filing them on shelves and in cabinets is an important part of a librarian's work, however the system used by librarians is quite standardized. Librarians learn how to organize materials according to a standard system used in libraries throughout the country.

Filing is an important responsibility for a secretary or a general office worker too, but the filing systems they use are not ordinarily standardized. The types of filing systems a secretary finds in an office when she begins to work may be inadequate or out of date. She may need to reorganize them, or she may need to develop a file for some new records. For this reason, office workers need a different kind of filing expertise.

This Workbook is for office workers. It gives them enough information and projects in handling typical office filing situations, especially correspondence and card files, so that they can confidently set up special-purpose office filing systems for managers and administrators of all kinds. This Workbook teaches the *fundamentals* of office filing systems especially for alphabetical correspondence files, geographic, subject, numeric, and date files.

Review Questions

1. Name two types of files kept in many homes.
2. Name three types of business files other than correspondence files.
3. What is the purpose of a file?
4. What is one of today's main filing problems?
5. Why does a secretary need to know something about filing?
6. Why should files be safeguarded?
7. Describe two ways files can be safeguarded.
8. Why is organization important in filing?
9. What is meant by organizing files?
10. What is the relation between organizing a file and classifying records?
11. What is the relation between organized office files and a business information system?
12. What important responsibilities do office workers in general have in developing and maintaining business information systems?

Projects

Project 1. *Vocabulary*

Purpose:

    1. To build an understanding of filing terminology.
    2. To add to your vocabulary.

Instructions:

    1. Find dictionary definitions for the following. Use an unabridged dictionary, if possible.
    2. Type the definitions neatly and hand them to your instructor for checking.

1.	file (and/or filing system)	6.	records
2.	classification	7.	control
3.	to organize	8.	maintain
4.	safeguard	9.	information
5.	memory	10.	alphabetical

Project 2. *Characteristic Records*

Match the record that you think best characterizes the job in the list below:

1.	Secretary	_____	A.	Ledgers
2.	Bookkeeper	_____	B.	Sales Slips
3.	Teacher	_____	C.	Reservations
4.	Banker	_____	D.	Inventory
5.	Librarian	_____	E.	Morgue
6.	News reporter	_____	F.	Checks
7.	Ticket office clerk	_____	G.	Notebooks
8.	Stationery supplies clerk	_____	H.	Periodicals
9.	Department store clerk	_____	I.	Grade Books
10.	Student	_____	J.	Correspondence

Project 3. *Information Files*

Purpose: To help you analyze the types of records and files people keep.

Instructions: Describe the items of information you think would be important in a file that contains records for one of the following situations:

1. A newscaster who has a different sponsor each day of the week except Sunday, when he doesn't broadcast.
2. Customer records in a local bakery shop that carries charge accounts.
3. An inventory and purchasing record in a local gas station.
4. A situation about which you personally know.

Project 4. *In the News*

Newspapers and similar communications media point out the importance of records, particularly in day-to-day activities. We read, for example, quotations such as the following:

> The prosecuting attorney noted from the files of the D. C. Lloyd Company that $5,000 were spent in entertainment expenses last year . . .

> Sales of the D. C. Lloyd Company reached its highest level since 1950 . . .

> Records in one of the offices of the D. C. Lloyd Company were almost totally destroyed by a fire last night . . .

Bring to class one newspaper article that implies the importance of records and explain why they are important.

2

Rules for Alphabetic Systems

Order is achieved in an alphabetical filing system by following an *a* to *z* sequence. The name *James* is filed ahead of *Jones* because the second letter in James (*a*) comes before the second letter in Jones (*o*) in the alphabet. Also, *Nelsen* is filed before *Nelson* because the fifth letter in Nelsen (*e*) comes before the fifth letter in Nelson (*o*), otherwise the two names are identical.

Each word, abbreviation, and initial in a name is a separate indexing unit unless otherwise identified by specific filing rules. Names are arranged in alphabetic order by comparing their units. If the first units in two different names are identical, consider the second unit. Use the third units when the first and second ones are identical.

	Correct Arrangement			
Name	*Unit 1*	*Unit 2*	*Unit 3*	*Unit 4*
Arnold Martin	Martin	Arnold		
Arnold J. Martin	Martin	Arnold	J	
Albert Morten	Morten	Albert		
Arnold Morten	Morten	Arnold		

At first glance, it seems that organizing a file alphabetically by name in an *a* to *z* sequence should be a simple system to use. Indeed, it is simple — until the file grows larger, the names get complicated, and inconsistencies in arrangement creep in. Unless consistency is maintained in the way names are filed, items get scattered in a file and are hard to find. For example, how should we file the John

7

McCabe & Sons' correspondence? Should it be filed under *J* for John, *M* for McCabe, or *S* for Sons? If we file it under the *M*, how should we file it in relation to other names? Straight alphabetic sequence? What about names that start with Mac? Should we put the *Macs* and the *Mcs* together? If we do not, we will have arrangements like the following, and some items may be hard to find:

Maattson	Magee
Mabaleen	Martin
MacAdam	McCabe

Another thing we must decide is when to file by a given first name and when by a family surname. We need some rules to follow in situations like the above to help us be consistent.

Standard Indexing Rules

Several different filing supply and equipment houses, filing experts, and the American Records Management Association (ARMA) have developed standard alphabetical indexing rules for name files. Unfortunately, there is not 100 percent agreement among these sets of rules.

Consistency

In its compilation of filing rules, ARMA calls attention to the fact that even when a basic rule is agreed to by all the "authorities," some inconsistency in application among companies may result because of personal choice. The Association suggests that a small file handled by only one person can be maintained without excessive concern about what is the most acceptable standard rule. In a large system, though, where several people work with the files, a set of rules should be agreed upon and followed consistently.

ARMA Rules

The American Records Management Association, a national association of filing and records management experts, appointed a committee to study alphabetical filing practices in modern business offices. One of the goals of the committee was to reconcile conflicts about rules. The ARMA committee reviewed alphabetical filing rules used in textbooks, in business and government filing manuals, and by compilers of dictionaries, encyclopedias, telephone books and directories. The rules presented in this Workbook are those endorsed by ARMA as a result of this study.

ARMA gives fifty-two rules for alphabetical filing. In this Workbook, these have been condensed into thirty rules, which are presented in four separate groups as follows:

Names	Number of Rules
A. Individual	7
B. Business	12
C. Institution	6
D. Government	5

A. Individual Names

Rule 1. Names of individuals are transposed so that the last name becomes the first indexing unit: last name, first name or initial, and middle name or initial.

Units

1	2	3
Brown,	Harold	
Brown,	Harold	E.
Brown,	Harold	Edward

1a. A surname with a first name but no middle initial precedes the same name with an initial. That is, *nothing comes before something.*

1	2
Brown	
Brown,	H.

1b. When the names of two or more individuals are identical, go to the name of the city, then the state, then the street name, and finally to the numeric order of the house numbers.

1	2	3	4	5	6
Ayers,	Dawn	Omaha,	Nebr.	Farnam Street	1827
Ayers,	Dawn	Omaha,	Nebr.	Farnam Street	4518

Rule 2.   Treat as part of the name, prefixes such as De, Du, La, Los, Mac, Mc, San, Van, etc., and file exactly as spelled. An exception is sometimes made of M', Mac, and Mc. Such names are sometimes filed together as a group at the beginning of the *M* section. When this is done, be consistent.

1	2	M's, Mc's, and Mac's Grouped	
de Bonneval,	Albert		
DeByle,	Jacqueline	MacNish,	Janie
Larue,	Charles	MacTavish,	Eileen
LaRue,	Walter	McAdam,	Cora
Lefevre,	Iris	M'Diera,	Sara
Macnee,	Tom		
MacNish,	Janie or	– – – – – – – – –	
MacTavish,	Eileen	Macnee,	Tom
McAdam,	Cora	Mazure,	Carole
M'Deira,	Sara	Meade,	Sarah
Van Dam,	Bud		
Van der Haas,	Kaye		
Van der Schalie,	Elaine		
Van Liere,	Sharon		

Rule 3.   Treat hyphenated last names as one complete unit.

Cuyler-Curtis, Hazel
Cuylerton, Paul

Rule 4.   When you cannot decide which is the last or the given name, file it as it occurs. Oriental names often fall into this classification. This type of name should be cross referenced.

	Cross Reference
Nhu Diem	Diem, Nhu (see Nhu Diem)
Vi-Cheng Liu	Liu, Vi-Cheng (see Vi-Cheng Liu)

Rule 5.   File abbreviations as though spelled in full *when the meaning is known.*

	Geo. Hayden	. . .	File: Hayden, George
but	Bud Lofton	. . .	Lofton, Bud

5a.   Treat firm endings such as Co., Inc., Bros., as a filing unit and as though spelled in full.

General Dynamics, Inc.(orporated)

5b.   File firm names as incorporated and spelled in full, not by a nicknamed version.

Full Name	Cross Reference to Nickname
American Medical Association	AMA
American Management Association	AMA
Columbia Broadcasting System	CBS

Rule 6.   The legal name of a married woman includes her own first name. If the husband's first name is known, her name *may be* cross referenced to his; *Mrs.* is put into parentheses at the end of the name

Logan, Lois E. (Mrs.) . . . Cross Reference: Logan, Richard G. (Mrs.)
See Logan, Lois E.

Rule 7.   University degrees and titles of distinction such as Professor, Doctor, Dean, and Captain when need for identification, are written after the name and considered as one filing unit. Otherwise they should be put into parentheses and disregarded.[1]

Walter Peterson, Ph.D.   File: Peterson, Walter (Ph.D.)

7a.   Titles that state seniority such as Sr., III (Third), 2nd, are used only when the names to be filed are otherwise identical. They are considered as an indexing unit at the end of the name.

7b.   Titles when followed by one name are filed as written.

Prince Philip, Queen Elizabeth.

---

[1] Some sources disregard titles entirely because they may or may not be used by the individuals themselves. Where they are disregarded and the names are otherwise identical, consider the city, state, and address as in Rule 1b.

Review Exercise 1

   a. Type (or write) the following names (last name first) on
      individual slips of paper or on 5″ by 3″ cards. This will
      make them easier to sort in alphabetical order.
   b. Alphabetize the cards.
   c. On an answer sheet like the one illustrated in Fig. 2–1,
      list the names in the proper alphabetical order. Opposite
      each name, indicate the rule(s) (2, 2a, etc.) which you
      used. Rule 1 need not be mentioned since it applies to
      each card.
   d. Hand the answer sheet* and the cards to the teacher for
      checking.

1. John E. Smith
2. Bill Van Devanter
3. Jane Mark-Durkee
4. William Doe
5. Mrs. Mary Smith
6. Dang Ng
7. Captain John Jones
8. John Smith, 1234 Elm Street,
            Baltimore, Md.
9. Jack Marketan
10. Smith
11. John Vanderwald
12. John Smith, 1222 Elm Street,
            Baltimore, Md.

ANSWER SHEET

Date _____

Student's Name _____

Assignment _(for example, Review Exercise 3, p 18)_____

Objectives: (for example–)

    1. Type cards
    2. Alphabetize
    3. Review rules for alphabetical name files
    4. Prepare answer sheet showing correct alphabetical sequence

Answers:

Figure 2-1. Answer sheet

*Make an appropriate answer sheet wherever one is requested in subsequent exercises,
using the heading shown in the answer sheet illustrated in Fig. 2-1.

Review Exercise 2

You work in the office of the manager of the electrical utilities company. He has a big correspondence file in his offices with drawers labeled as shown below. On an answer sheet, write the number of the drawer in which each one of the following would be filed. For example: file 1 would be in drawer 4.

Aa-Ao 1	Bl-Bz 4	Daa-Doa 7	Er-Ez 10	Ga-Gq 13	Heo-Hz 16	Ka-Kom 19	Loa-Lz 22
Ap-Az 2	Caa-Coo 5	Dob-Dz 8	Fa-Fq 11	Gra-Gz 14	I-Jn 17	Kon-Kz 20	Maa-Mn 23
Baa-Bk 3	Cop-Cz 6	Ea-Eq 9	Fr-Fz 12	Haa-Hen 15	Jo-Jz 18	Laa-Ln 21	Mo-Mz 24

Correspondence files

1. Mrs. Mario Buccellati
2. Dennis Horowitz
3. Vincent Finn and Son
4. Mrs. Lolita Roche Diaze
5. Henry Csigay
6. Barney Cuccioli
7. Hayes Malcolm
8. Michael Malge
9. Helen Hayes
10. J. C. McWade
11. Miss Belle Meachim
12. Mathew McO'Neal
13. J. G. McOrlly
14. Al Horswell
15. Karl Fink, M.C.
16. Mary Bubniak
17. Benjamin Cooper
18. Mrs. Bessie Cooper
19. L. O. Combs
20. Hattie M. Malcolm

B. Business Names

Rule 1.   When a firm name is made up of the name of an individual plus other words, transpose the individual's name.

> Robert W. Bahr Furniture Stores, Inc.
>
> File: Bahr, Robert W. Furniture Stores, Inc.

Exception: When a firm name that includes an individual's name becomes so well known that to reverse it would cause confusion, file the name as it is.

> Mark Cross and Company
> Marshall Field and Company

Rule 2.   When a firm name contains the full names of two or
              more individuals, file by the name of the first person
              mentioned and cross reference to the others.

	John Tracy, Bruce Smythe, and Howard Hanson, Consultants, Inc.
File:	Tracy, John (Bruce Smythe and Howard Hanson) Consultants, Inc.
Cross Reference:	Smythe, Bruce (see Tracy, John and Howard Hanson) Consultants, Inc.
	Hanson, Howard (see Tracy, John and Smythe, Bruce) Consultants, Inc.

Rule 3.   File coined or trade names as *one* unit since they are
              often parts of words with unusual spellings.

Units:	1	2	3
	Hi Note	Music	Suppliers
	Hinote	Cafe	
	New-Way	Cafe	
	Klip-U-Rite	Pet	Shop
	Stop-A-While	Restaurant	

Rule 4.   When individual names are hyphenated to form one firm
              name, treat them as separate filing units.

Units:	1	2	3
	Prentice-	Hall,	Inc.

Rule 5.   When single letters make up a company name, file them
              as separate units.

Units:	1	2	3	4	5	6
	A	B	C	School	Supplies	Inc.
	Triple	A	Accountants	Inc.		

5a.   Each letter in the name of a radio or television station is
         filed as a separate unit.

Units:	1	2	3	4	5
	W	J	R	Radio	Station

Rule 6.   Treat each word in a compound geographical firm name
         as a separate filing unit, except when the first part of
         the name is not an English word such as San in San
         Francisco.

Units:	1	2	3	4
	New	York	State	Bank
	St.	Peters	Resort	Retreat
	San Francisco	Restaurant	Association	
	United	States	Steel	Corporation

Rule 7.   Treat each word in a firm name containing compass
         points as a separate filing unit.[2] Cross reference may be
         needed for clarification.

Units:	1	2	3	4	Cross Reference
	North	Western	Railroad		(See also Northwestern)
	South	Western	Publishing	Company	(See also Southwestern)

Rule 8.   Put into parentheses and disregard articles, conjunctions,
         or prepositions that are part of a firm name such as *and,
         for, in, of, the, a, an.*

Units:		1		2		3	4
(The)		New		York		State	Bank
		St.		Peters	(a)	Resort	Retreat
		Top (of the)		Mark		Hotel	

---

[2] Many filing books suggest the opposite — that firm names containing compass points be
treated as one unit. Whichever practice is adopted, it should be followed consistently.

Exceptions: When a foreign article meaning *a, an,* or *the* is the initial word of a business name, the name is filed as written.

Units:	1	2	3
	LaSalle	Street	Station

Rule 9. Consider everything up to the apostrophe; disregard the 's.[3]

		File:	
Johnston's			Johnston
Johnstone's			Johnstone
Johnstons'			Johnstons

9a. Disregard the apostrophe in elisions and file the word as spelled without it.

Units:	1	2	3	4
	What's (Whats)	My	Line	Program
	Here's (Heres)	How	Products	Inc.

9b. Disregard accentual, diacritical, and foreign-word markings and file the words as written.

Olan Osterbaüm   File: Osterbaüm, Olan

Rule 10. When numbers are part of a firm name, file as though spelled in full.

Units:	1	2	3
	(The) Eighteen	Club	
	Heinz	Fifty-seven	Varieties
	(The) Twentieth	Century	Limited

10a. Numbers of three and four digits are read as hundreds, and the number is filed as one unit.

---

[3] ARMA recommends disregarding the apostrophe and filing the word as written. Thus Johnstone's would be filed as Johnstones. This rule is consistent with Rule 9a, but the authors do not recommend it.

Units:	*1*	*2*	*3*
(The) 1406	Golf	Club	(Fourteen hundred and six)

10b. Numbers of five or more digits are read as thousands, hundred thousands, or millions and the number is filed as one unit: 25,000 (twenty-five thousand); 7,000,000 (seven million). If a title contains several inclusive numbers, file by the lowest number.

18–21 Club, Inc.   File: Eighteen (twenty-one) Club Inc.

Rule 11. When a parent company and subsidiaries are involved, file by the name of the parent or holding company but cross reference to the subsidiaries, divisions, or affiliates. *Poor's Register of Directors and Executives* and *Moody's Industrial Manual* will aid in clarifying interrelations among companies, but the best authority for the main name by which to file is a company's own letterhead or forms such as invoices and purchase orders.

Parent	*Subsidiaries*
McGraw Edison Company:	Thomas A. Edison Industries Toastmaster Division

11a. When communications relate to transactions with individuals or particular departments in a firm, file by the name of the firm. Cross reference to the name of the individual, the department, or the project title if necessary.

D. C. Buras, Administrative Methods Department,
    General Dynamics, Inc.
File: General Dynamics, Inc. (Cross reference if necessary.)

Rule 12. When the name of a foreign firm is written in English, file according to the usual rules. But if it is not in English, file exactly as written. If you can translate, cross reference.

File: Guias Scouts de Colombia
Cross Reference: (See Scouts, Girls of Colombia SA.
                Also see Colombia (South America)
                Girl Scouts

Review Exercise 3

    a. Type the following names on 5" by 3" cards. Type the number of the name in the upper right corner of the card.

    b. Alphabetize the cards.

    c. On an answer sheet like the one used in Review Exercise 1, write the numbers of the items and the numbers of the rules that apply.

    d. Make sure to prepare any necessary cross-reference cards.

    e. Hand the answer sheet and the cards (including cross-reference cards) to the teacher for checking.

1. Harry H. Richards Furniture Stores, Inc.
2. Marshall Field and Company
3. Fix-It Appliance Shop
4. Prentice-Hall, Inc.
5. K.B.J. Radio Station
6. New Jersey Road Equipment, Inc.
7. Northwestern Railroad Company
8. North Carolina Power Company, Raleigh Division
9. The San Diego Zoo Company
10. The What's My Line Program
11. The Twenty-One Club
12. The World's Finest Chocolates, Inc.
13. Ninos Scouts de Mexico
14. St. Paul's Cathedral
15. Rest Easy Mattress Company, Inc.

C. Institution Names

Rule 1.   File churches, hospitals, colleges, banks, chambers of commerce, and so on under the first distinctive word in the title. If the name does not contain a distinctive word, file under the name of the city or state.

(The) University of Michigan	File: Michigan (The) University (of)
First National Bank of Monroe	Monroe, First National Bank (of)
Saint Luke's Methodist Church	Methodist, St. Luke's Church

In large files, such items might first be grouped under subject guides: *University, Bank,* or *Church.*

Rule 2.   When filing hotel and motel names, reverse the name if necessary so that the most significant word comes first. Add location where possible, to identify the unit further.

Hotel Statler	File: Statler Hotel (Chicago)
Stage Coach Motel	Stage Coach Motel (Detroit)

If a hotel is part of a well-known chain and this is not indicated in the name of the hotel, it may be helpful to include the name of the chain.

Hotel Georgian, Evanston, Ill.
File: Georgian (Pick Chain) Hotel, Evanston, Ill.

Rule 3.   When the same name appears with different addresses, file by location. If, however, the file is limited to the local unit of the organization only, file by the title.

Cross Reference

Dearborn, Young Men's Christian Association	(See YMCA)
Detroit, Young Men's Christian Association	(See YMCA)
Flint, Young Men's Christian Association	(See YMCA)
Kalamazoo, Young Men's Christian Association	(See YMCA)

Rule 4.   File public schools under the city of location followed by Education (Board of) and distinctive school names.[4]

Aloha High School, Beaverton, Ore.
File: Beaverton (Oregon) School District, Aloha High School

Rule 5.   File newspapers, magazines, and chain stores under their distinctive titles.

Units:	1	2	3	4
	Wall	Street	Journal	
	Harvard	Business	Review	
	New	York	Times	
	Red (and)	White	Stores	Inc.

[4] Actual practices for listing schools vary considerably. Check your telephone directory. Several list schools in the classified directory as "Schools – Public, Private & Parochial, Colleges & Universities." Under this heading, all the schools are listed alphabetically according to the first significant word of the title. City schools are grouped under the name of the city.

Rule 6.   File estates and guardianships under the names of the principals. Cross reference to the name of the guardian, trustee, or administrator.

> Estate of Nelly Krance
> File: Krance, Nelly (Estate of). See Archer, Robert, Administrator

Review Exercise 4

a. Define each of the following. Use a dictionary if necessary. Type your definitions.
b. Hand the definitions to the teacher for checking. Write your name, the date, and the exercise number on the sheet.

1. ARMA
2. Compound name
3. Filing unit
4. Filing rules
5. Coined word
6. Diacritical

Review Exercise 5

a. Find the misfiled item(s) in each of the following groups.
b. Show the correct sequence on an answer sheet, referring to the items by the numbers and letters used below.
c. Hand the answer sheet to the teacher for checking.

1. (a) The Uhde Corporation
   (b) George Uhe Company, Inc.
   (c) Señor Juan Uhkiv
2. (a) Mascot's Stores
   (b) Mascot, Emma
   (c) Mask-O-Neg Co.
3. (a) Arima Trading Assn.
   (b) Ari-Even, Mathew
   (c) Arimex Importers, Inc.
4. (a) A & B Auto Rental Service
   (b) Ab Bender's Binding Corp.
   (c) The AB Radio Station

5. (a)   A-One Furniture Store
   (b)   A-1 Sprinkler System
   (c)   A-1 Answering Service
6. (a)   A & P Food Stores
   (b)   A P Chemicals
   (c)   A. P. Little Consultants, Inc.
7. (a)   The 9-4 Avenue Club
   (b)   Fourth Avenue Gift Shop
   (c)   The 18 Club
8. (a)   1814 Amsterdam Cafe
   (b)   1804 Second Avenue Corporation
   (c)   18 East 45th Street Club
9. (a)   Neoberg Furs
   (b)   Neo-Art Studio
   (c)   Neopolitan Opera Company
10. (a)   The University of New Mexico
    (b)   The Union Club
    (c)   Novelty Gift Shop

Review Exercise 6

a. Underline the first indexing unit in each of the following names.

b. Type the names in alphabetical sequence with the first indexing unit in all capitals.

c. After each name, indicate in parentheses the number(s) of the rule(s) used. Also, indicate cross references, if any.

d. Give the exercise a title.

e. Hand it to the teacher for checking.

1. The University of Washington
2. Hunter College, New York
3. The Thunderbird Motel, Detroit, Mich.
4. The First Presbyterian Church, Portland
5. La Paloma Apartments
6. The Delta Pi Epsilon Journal
7. Estate of Maggie Krance (Austin Ames, Administrator)
8. Young Women's Christian Assn., Seattle
9. The Benson Hotel, Portland, Oregon
10. Leo Parmerton Industries, Inc.

D. Government names

Rule 1. A breakdown should be made under a main heading –
for example, United States Government – according to
distinctive words in the name of the subsidiary bureau
or unit.

1	2	3
United States Government	Commerce (Department of)	Weather Bureau
	Federal Aviation Agency	Air Carrier Safety Aircraft Engineering Airport Traffic Hdqts. General Aviation Systems Maintenance
	Post Office	Main Office
	Selective Service	Local Board

Rule 2. For state or local agencies, file by the state, county, or
city, following with the distinctive name of the organizational unit. The words *state of, county of, city of,* and so
on are added for clarity and *ARE* considered as filing
units. Words such as *Bureau of, Board of,* and *Commis-
sion of* are put into parentheses and are *NOT* considered
in filing.

	1	2	3	4
State of New Hampshire, Department of Highways	File: New	Hampshire	State of	Highways (Department of)
New York, N.Y. Department of Finance	New	York	City	Finance (Department of)

Rule 3. Armed Forces camps and bases are filed under an identifying word in the title since the specific department or

branch to which they report is not always known, nor is an outlying camp necessarily associated with a nearby city.

Fort Crook Training Center
Fort Knowles Camp
Wright Paterson Airfield

Rule 4.   Committees, commissions, and government projects are often referred to by initials. File by the name in full when it is known and cross reference to the initials.

	Cross Reference
File: Federal Housing Administration	(See FHA)

Rule 5.   Foreign governments are filed according to the same logic as that used for the United States. The identifying name of the country always comes first.

Department of the Interior for the Commonwealth of
    Great Britain
File: England, Interior (Department of)

A cross reference to *Commonwealth* might show:

See, Commonwealth of Great Britain: Australia, Canada,
    New Zealand, etc.

The *World Almanac and Book of Facts* is a helpful source for clarification of foreign government titles. A copy of the *United States Government Organizational Manual* is a good reference for names of U.S. government branches, executive departments, committees, and commissions. It is prepared by the Federal Register Division, National Archives and Records Service, General Services Administration, Washington, D.C.

Discussion Questions

1. Why did the American Records Management Association form a committee to study practices in alphabetic filing?
2. Why do we need to standardize filing rules?

3. What are some differences between filing company names and individual names?
4. What are some differences between filing government names and individual names?
5. What would you do if you worked in an office that used filing rules that differed from those recommended by the American Records Management Association?

Review Exercise 7

a. On an answer sheet, indicate the correct filing sequence for the following names.
b. Indicate the filing rules that apply.
c. Hand the answer sheet to the instructor for checking.

1. Martin-Clinton Corporation
2. Ann Arbor Clothing Store
3. O and H Garage
4. East Side Auto Parts
5. O K Auto Service
6. Paul's Musical Repair Shop
7. Northwest Pipe & Supply Company
8. Union Savings Bank of Manchester
9. National Bank of Ypsilanti
10. Slaussen Public High School, Albion, Ohio

Project 1. *Updating Subscriptions*

Purpose: This project aims to give you experience in:

1. Handling a subscription file;
2. Applying the indexing rules for alphabetical name systems;
3. Updating a file.

Instructions:

1. Assume that the following 40 items are characteristic of the entire subscription file. Put the items into alphabetical sequence.
2. Type the list, doubled-spaced, with the first indexing unit in all capitals.

3. Make the 30 additions and corrections by typing them in between the lines. Use longhand where necessary.
4. Hand the list to the instructor for checking. Did you give the list a title?
5. When this project is returned, save it. The names will be used again in Project 2, Chapter 7.

The File

1. Mrs. Mario Buccellati, 705 Plaza Street, Black Hills, South Dakota
2. Dennis Horowitz, 277 First Avenue, New York, New York
3. Vincent Finn and Son, One Madison Street, Cleveland, Ohio
4. Mrs. Lolita Roche Diaze, 17 Sherwood Road, Ypsilanti, Michigan
5. The Culver Fabrics Shop, 4518 So. 69th Street, San Antonio, Texas
6. Henry Csigay, 1543 Marlboro Blvd., Superior, Wisconsin
7. The Eastside Methodist Church, 70-74 Carling Blvd., Minneapolis, Minnesota
8. Barney Cuccioli, 60 Riverside Drive, Freeport, Maine
9. Camp Na-Wa-Kwa, Sheridan Lane, Bangor, Maine
10. Hayes Malcolm, Manhattan Drive, Fort Lauderdale, Florida
11. Michael Malge, Corning Road, Orange, Texas
12. The Maline Associates, Inc., 4633 Tower Building, San Francisco, California
13. The Ponce DeLeon Hotel, Fairfield, Florida
14. Smilow-Thielle Furniture, 1860 Cresset, Chicago, Illinois
15. The United Ignition Corporation, 11352 Chambers Building, Detroit, Michigan
16. The United Nations Mission (Pakistan), 8 East 65th Street, NE, Washington, D.C.
17. United States Academy Motel, Highland Falls Road, Arlington, Virginia
18. Office of the Auditor General, United States Air Force, 641 Washington Street, New York City
19. United States Coast Guard Base, St. George Bay, Long Island, New York

20. Administrative Office, National Aeronautics and Space Administration, Western Division, Olympia, Washington
21. Harkness Naval Base, Floyd Bennett Field, Brooklyn, New York
22. Wright Paterson Air Force Base, Columbus, Ohio
23. The National Bank of Pueblo, Pueblo, Colorado
24. US Projector Corporation, WOW Building, Des Moines, Iowa
25. J. C. McWade, Hanson Blvd., Albuquerque, New Mexico
26. Miss Belle Meachim, Gold River Drive, Fairfield, Connecticut
27. Mathew McO'Neal, Greview Road, Long Beach, California
28. The In Friendship Cafe, Commerce Building, Philadelphia, Pennsylvania
29. The In-Tag Suppliers, 18285 Archer Building, Dallas, Texas
30. J. G. McOrlly, 4200 East Washington, Butte, Montana
31. McSorels Old Timers Inn, Galesburg, Illinois
32. Al Horswell, 4829 South Blvd., Beverly Hills, California
33. Karl Fink, M.D., 140 Medical Center, Boston, Massachusetts
34. Mary Bubniak, Professor of History, University of Nebraska, Lincoln, Nebraska
35. Mrs. Shirley Buchalter, West End Avenue, Beacon Hill, Massachusetts
36. Jack Adams, M.D., 14 Hilton Road, Bradford, Pennsylvania
37. The Abrons House, Miller, Nebraska
38. The Academy of American Poets, 1078 Madison Avenue, Shelby, North Carolina
39. Cooper-Bessemer Corporation, General Offices, Scranton, Pennsylvania
40. Geneno Brothers, Realtors, Acme Building, Jacksonville, Florida

Corrections

1. Change spelling of Buccellati to Bencelloti
2. Change address of In-Tag Suppliers to 2744 Harcourt Building, Houston, Texas

3. Change McWade subscription to Mrs. John McWade, Tower Apartments
4. Change Belle Meachim subscription to 88 Phillips, Bridgeport, Connecticut
5. Change spelling of Abrons House, Miller, Nebraska to Abrown House

Additions

6. George Fink Industries, Satlow Drive, Fort Atkinson, Wisconsin
7. General Offices, Adam's Brush Company, 14 Mullett Drive, Lynwood, California
8. Academy Tours, 29 Regal Road, New Orleans, Louisiana
9. Benjamin Cooper, 3177 Fagen Street, Charleston, West Virginia
10. General Aerospace Materials Suppliers, 7784 Walton Street, Nashville, Tennessee
11. Mrs. Bessie Cooper, Forest Plaza Apartments, Portland, Oregon
12. Adams Book Company, Union Building, New Orleans, Louisiana
13. Horological Works, Inc., 15 Castle Building, Richmond, Virginia
14. Hornkohl Greenhouses, Shady Road, Little Rock, Arkansas
15. Kriwow Farms, Inc., Denver, Colorado
16. Children's Clinic, US Department of Health, Education and Welfare, Baltimore, Maryland
17. Highway Transportation Study Headquarters, N.Y. Metropolitan Region, 201 Park Avenue, New York, New York
18. Roland Walton, 731 Amsterdam Avenue, Miami, Florida
19. Robert Rogoff, 691 State Building, Duluth, Minnesota
20. Jo Ann Weber, 269 Utica, Boise, Idaho
21. Lawrence Webster, Penobscot Building, Reno, Nevada
22. Youth Placement Service, Sickle Arcade, Oklahoma City, Oklahoma
23. Young Women's Christian Assn. of the USA, Providence, Rhode Island

24. Werner Zinke, M.D., Medical Center, Birmingham, Alabama
25. Theo. Quarg, 105 Mill Road, Scranton, Pennsylvania

Project 2. *An Achievement Test in Alphabetical Filing*

Purpose: The objective of this project is to

1. check your knowledge of the alphabetical indexing rules;
2. check your ability to alphabetize accurately.

Instructions:

1. On an answer sheet, write the letter (*a, b, c,* or *d*) that identifies the name that should be filed *last* in each of the following series.
2. Hand the answer sheet to the instructor for checking.

1. (a)   MaryJane Johnson
   (b)   Mary Johnston
   (c)   Marie Jane Johnston
   (d)   Marianne Johnson
2. (a)   University of Oregon
   (b)   U S National Bank of Oregon
   (c)   Oregon Hilton Hotel
   (d)   Portland (Oregon) Secretarial School
3. (a)   Hilton Washington Hotel
   (b)   University of Washington
   (c)   The National Bank of Washington
   (d)   Washington Banking School
4. (a)   James MacCrea
   (b)   J. B. McCrea
   (c)   The Mac Crea Shoe Stores
   (d)   Macreal Sporting Goods
5. (a)   The 500 Club
   (b)   10-Hour Cleaners
   (c)   4-Points Motel
   (d)   The 20th Century Science Foundation
6. (a)   Friar Jim's Lunch Room
   (b)   Father Jerald
   (c)   Father's Motor Hotel
   (d)   The Friars Seminary

7. (a)   The Northwest Travel Agency
   (b)   The North West Airlines
   (c)   Great Northern Lumber Company
   (d)   Eileen North (Mrs. Wesley)
8. (a)   Arizona Holiday Motor Hotel
   (b)   Arnold Plumbing Company
   (c)   Arnold's Petroleum Service
   (d)   Arnold's Ski Shop
9. (a)   Emily Beeson O'Neal
   (b)   Eunice O'Neal (Mrs. Edward)
   (c)   ONEAL's Body Shop
   (d)   E. E. O'Neil
10. (a)   Sara Sutherland (Mrs. Stanley)
    (b)   S C M Corporation
    (c)   Sutton Electrostatic Dry Copier
    (d)   Copyright Service
11. (a)   Safe-Way Crown Cleaning
    (b)   S. A. Waring
    (c)   School of Custom Dress Design
    (d)   The Seeing-Eye School of Seattle
12. (a)   Prince Phillip
    (b)   Rose Festival Queen
    (c)   General George Mitchell
    (d)   Bishop John Keaning
13. (a)   USSR
    (b)   USA
    (c)   Dominion of Canada
    (d)   Republic of France
14. (a)   Arizona State College at Tempe
    (b)   The State University of Arizona
    (c)   Austin Peasy State College
    (d)   Pasadena School of the Sacred Heart
15. (a)   California School of Fine Arts
    (b)   California State College at Long Beach
    (c)   California Maritime Academy
    (d)   University of California Medical Center
16. (a)   Donald C. Underwood, II
    (b)   D. C. Underwood, III
    (c)   D. Underwood, Jr.
    (d)   D. Carl Underwood, Sr.
17. (a)   Hahnemann Medical Center
    (b)   Hampden-Sydney College
    (c)   Hampden-Sydney Community College
    (d)   Adolph Hamilton Medical Center

18. (a) New Jersey Women's College
    (b) Mt. St. Joseph Teachers College
    (c) Misericordia Community College
    (d) Mary Washington College at Lexington
19. (a) University of North Dakota
    (b) Northern Illinois University
    (c) Northern School of Mines
    (d) The City University of New York
20. (a) United Church Training School
    (b) Military Academy at West Point, New York
    (c) United States Naval Postgraduate School
    (d) United University

3

Office Filing Practices

To maintain an efficient system, certain practices should be standardized. Efficient filing is the result of standardized practices in the following activities: (1) collecting, (2) conditioning, (3) inspecting, (4) indexing and coding, (5) cross referencing, (6) sorting, (7) filing, and (8) retrieving.

1. Collecting

Each day, collect materials for the files by batching them at a certain location at your work station, either in an out-box, a special drawer, or a special location on a nearby shelf or file. Items to be filed will include folders, letters, forms, and reports. Efficient accumulation depends on how carefully you follow your routine and on how well you train yourself to put items into your filing "batch" as you handle them during the day. It also depends on how well you train your boss not to hoard papers. You should convince him that they will be waiting for him when he wants them if they are properly filed.

General Rule
Arrange papers into related groupings (folders, cases, or projects) when possible, as this is the easiest way to file and find information.

2. Conditioning

Remove all pins, brads, paper clips, and rubber bands from materials. Staple outgoing correspondence with related incoming papers and handle them *as a unit*. Staple together papers that go as a unit. The preferred spot for a staple is diagonally across the upper left-hand corner, but eventually an accumulation of these will cause a bulge in the left corner. For this reason, it is a good practice to alternate staples between the right and left corners to prevent their becoming too bulky.

Attach loose clippings or small items of related materials (less than 8½″ by 11″ in size, particularly 5″ by 3″ and 6″ by 4″ slips and cards) to a regular sheet of paper by stapling or gluing. Mend or reinforce damaged records with tape.

> *General Rule*
>
> Staple papers that belong together so that they do not accidently become attached to other papers.

If a document to be filed does not have a title, give it one that will help you find and recognize it later.

If an item is oversize and cannot be folded (for example, a poster), file it separately in suitable equipment and cross reference it to the regular file.

> *General Rule*
>
> Bulky or odd-sized materials that do not fit easily into a filing system should be cross referenced and stored in an appropriate location.

3. Inspecting

Check documents for filing release. The release mark is the authority to file. It may appear in one of several different forms: the writer's initials, the word "file" written on the document, or a diagonal line across the sheet. If the release mark is not there, return the paper to the writer. Carbon copies of outgoing items ordinarily do not require release marks.

> *General Rule*
>
> Check papers for release marks that indicate they are ready to file. Unless this is done, there is no assurance that a paper has been seen and acted on.

Check attachments to the various documents to see if they belong there. If you can tell that an attachment that should be with a document is missing, mark the document "Attachment missing" and return it to the boss. Never file uncashed checks or money orders.

Unnecessary material such as extra copies, preliminary rough drafts, memos that have served their purpose, and correspondence about hotel reservations for trips already taken should be screened out to prevent overloading files with useless items.

> *General Rule*
>
> Wherever an organized filing system is used, someone should have the *authority* to decide which items to file and which to throw away.

4. Indexing and Coding

Some filing authorities differentiate between indexing and coding. *Indexing* is deciding under what name, subject, or caption an item is to be filed. For example, when indexing a letter, you need to decide whether the item will be indexed by the name of the:

a. writer or signer
b. company letterhead
c. person addressed

d. a person or subject discussed in the letter
e. location

Coding is actually marking on the paper, by a checkmark, an underline, or by encircling a word, the indexing caption decided upon. Indexing is a mental decision, whereas coding is the physical action of marking. Since the two steps are performed almost simultaneously, they are considered here as one activity.

> ### General Rule
>
> Index document files so material can be *found* when needed. Keep index captions short and clear.

Read a record carefully in order to find the correct indexing caption. Code it clearly and accurately. Sometimes items need to be cross referenced because correspondence and related documents are filed under other captions. Such items should be sorted out (batched) and the cross reference made at one time. Rubber finger tips speed up the handling of papers.

5. Cross Referencing[1]

A cross reference is a filing entry under an indexing caption other than the primary one that tells you where the document to which it refers is filed. Cross referencing requires putting sheets in places where people might look for a document or file. Some items may be called for by several different names, making it at times hard to tell just where to look for them in the files. The value of cross referencing is that it helps you find items quickly after they are requested. Two types of cross-reference systems — the item cross-reference sheet and the permanent cross-reference — are illustrated in Figs. 3–1 and 3–2.

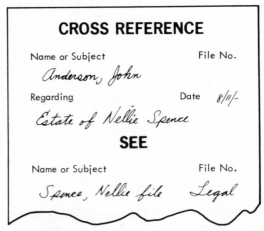

CROSS REFERENCE

Name or Subject   File No.

Anderson, John

Regarding   Date   *8/11/-*

Estate of Nellie Spence

SEE

Name or Subject   File No.

Spence, Nellie file   Legal

Figure 3–1. Item cross-reference sheet

---

[1] See Chapter 10, Maintaining and Controlling Filing Systems, for more about cross referencing.

File the cross-reference form under the name given at the top of the sheet. Describe the contents for identification purposes. The main file should be accumulated under the name given after SEE. Color code the cross-reference sheet using blue, green, pink, or yellow stationery.

Figure 3-2. A permanent cross reference

A permanent cross reference is a fixed part of a filing system and is typed on a folder or a guide. It should even be moved with files when they are transferred to storage.

Cross references are used whenever a record refers to more than one person, subject, or company. They eliminate guesswork and nail down the total reference picture. *When needed,* prepare a separate cross-reference sheet (see Fig. 3-1) or use a photocopy or an extra copy (of a distinctive color marked "Cross Reference"). An individual cross-reference sheet shows

a. The date of the item being cross referenced;
b. The name or subject of the item;
c. A description of what the item is about;
d. The name or subject under which the original paper is filed.

General Rules

A copy of a document is preferable to a cross-reference form because it provides the full text.

Restrict cross referencing to only those situations in which it is absolutely necessary.

---

6. Sorting

Sorting is the orderly arrangement of the coded papers into *a* through *z* sequence before they are put into the files. Papers are sorted by the indexing caption that has been marked, preferably with a colored pencil, on the record.

General Rule

Presort papers for filing. This practice saves filing time.

Where papers cannot be filed daily, they at least should be inspected, indexed, coded, and put into a sorting tray with guides. Here they will be kept in filing order so that possible requests for them before they are filed can be handled easily. If a sorting tray is not available, sort papers on a table or desk top. A routine such as the following saves time:

a. Sort the papers into alphabetical piles such as A-F, G-L, M-R, S-Z. This procedure is called rough sorting.
b. Fine sort each pile. For example, the A-F division should be separated into six piles: *A, B, C, D, E,* and *F.*
c. Alphabetize the papers within each pile.
d. Assemble all the papers for actual filing.

7. Filing

This step is the actual placing of items into file containers such as folders. The routine for filing items into vertical drawer files is as follows:

a. Hook a filing shelf onto the handle of the drawer nearest the one into which you will file next.
b. Place items to be filed on the shelf.
c. Read the filing code on the next paper to be filed.
d. Locate the drawer by reading the label.
e. Open the drawer and scan the guides and folder tabs, starting at the front, until you locate the desired folder.

f. Raise the folder and open it. When raising a folder in a file drawer, grasp it in the center, not by the tab. Pulling folders up by their tabs is hard on the tab and may tear the folder.

g. Compare the tab with the coded caption to make sure you have the right folder.

h. Put the paper into the folder with the heading to the left as it faces you.

If you do not find an individual folder with the desired name, put the item into the miscellaneous folder for that section. When you do so, check to see if five or more papers have accumulated for the name. If they have, make a folder for it. (See Chapter 10, Maintaining and Controlling Filing Systems.)

i. After the filing for a drawer has been completed, the "follower" at the back of the drawer should be brought up as tightly as possible. This keeps the drawer contents from sagging or slumping.

> *General Rule*
>
> Use labor-saving devices wherever possible.

Some Time-Saving Ideas

Use labor-, time-, and energy-saving devices whenever possible — a hook-on shelf for drawer and shelf files, a low stool when filing in bottom drawers, a tall stool when filing in high drawers, a rubber finger tip to aid in riffling through papers. Set a definite time for filing each day.

For drawer files

File records face up, top edge of the document to the left, with most recent date on the top except in miscellaneous and numeric files.

Place individual folders immediately *behind* the guide.

Place a Miscellaneous folder at the end of each section of the file, just in front of the next guide. When five records relating to one topic accumulate in the Miscellaneous folder, open an individual folder.

Use a guide for every 6–8 folders (1 inch of drawer space), about 20–25 per drawer.

Leave one-fifth of the drawer, at least 4 inches, for expansion and working space.

Keep 20–25 sheets in one folder. Beyond that, use scored folders (with creases at the bottom), folding along the creases for expansion purposes. The papers then rest more evenly on the bottom of the folder, the folders have a base on which to stand, and the folders can hold up to 100 sheets.

"Break" the files when the folder contains more than 100 pieces or ¾ inch. Make a new folder for the most recent records. Underscore the caption on the old folder in red so that all new material will be placed in the new folder. The first folder might be labelled January 1973–July 1974 and the second folder would have the date July 1974– in addition to its usual caption.

Use folders with pockets for bulky samples, swatches, or catalogs, with the same cut as the other folders.

Use pressure-sensitive labels. Remove the backing strip and apply just below the top edge of the folder tab. Press over the entire label so that all corners are tight.

Work from the side of the file rather than from the front. There is less strain on the worker this way.

Avoid accidents by opening only one file drawer at a time. Close a drawer as soon as a filing job has been completed.

When handling a folder, lift it up and rest it part-way on the side of the drawer. This enables you to insert documents easily and neatly without losing your place in the file.

Do not grasp guides and folders by the index tab. They are easier to handle and their life is prolonged if they are fingered from the center or the sides.

Use both hands for inserting and pulling out folders and correspondence.

General Rule

File daily. When filing is not kept up-to-date, time is wasted looking for papers that are supposed to be in the files.

8. Retrieving

Retrieving is finding. In every office there is a constant need for things from the files. A goal of every filing system is to enable people to find any item when it is wanted. There is not much point to keeping records if they cannot be found when wanted.

If the above filing steps are followed carefully, you should be able to find the great majority of papers requested. Misfiles and hard-to-find records are frequently caused by the following:

a. Drawers are overcrowded so that there is not enough work space either for filing or finding.
b. Folders are overloaded.
c. Tabs are frayed or faded.
d. Paper clips pick up papers and attach them to batches where they don't belong.
e. Papers are not properly cross referenced.
f. The paper was filed incorrectly — either before or after the folder it was intended for, or in between folders.
g. The paper was incorrectly indexed and coded.
h. An untrained person used the files.

The following suggestions may help you locate a paper when it has been misfiled:

a. If only one paper is lost, the chances are that it is in the wrong folder. Check the folder in front, and in back, and look on the bottom of the drawer.
b. Look in the sorter.
c. Look under other possible indexing units.
d. If an entire folder is misfiled, look in
   1. your desk, especially the out-basket
   2. the boss's desk and out-basket
   3. folders with similar names
   4. the transferred files
   5. the charge-out file.

Review Questions

1. An employee in central files said, "Cross referencing can be both a boon and a headache." What did she mean?

2. If your employer asked you to get a letter from Harry Smith from a project file and you could not find it, what would you do? If you eventually found it in the top drawer of your employer's desk, what would you say?
3. Why is a release mark used on documents to be filed?
4. Why should correspondence be filed every day?
5. What does "conditioning" items for filing involve?
6. Describe the basic steps in preparing papers for filing.
7. What is coding? How does it differ from indexing?
8. Describe the methods for coding a business letter.
9. What is the procedure for selecting an indexing caption?
10. Describe five ways to save time and energy in filing.

Review Exercise 1

a. Prepare an answer sheet suitable for recording the answers to this exercise.
b. Read the following statements and indicate by a *C* on your answer sheet those items that you consider to be good filing practices. If you do not agree with the item, do not put a letter on the answer sheet after the number of the statement. Be prepared to discuss in class *why* you thought a statement did or did not describe a good filing practice.
c. Hand the answer sheet to the instructor for checking.

1. When an item to be filed covers more than one subject, name, etc., cross reference by the subjects and names that are most likely to be used when the item is requested.
2. Make an extra carbon copy or a photocopy of an item that is to be cross referenced.
3. Mark cross-referenced copies to indicate who signed the cross-reference sheet.
4. When your boss fails to release an item for the files by initialing it, you may do it for him.
5. Rough sort items in the same sequence as the file tab guides in which the papers are to be placed.
6. Fasten items together with a staple when you are reasonably certain they will be asked for in that way.

7. Avoid using color coding in filing systems because it gets confusing.
8. When you have oversized or bulky material to file, cross reference it.
9. It is not necessary to keep your filing up to date.
10. Have your boss turn papers over to you to file.
11. It is all right to let anyone who wishes use your files.
12. File copies of form or routine letters do not have to be made.

Review Exercise 2

   a. Prepare an answer sheet suitable for recording the answers to this exercise.
   b. After each descriptive statement, write the number of the term in the list on the left that fits the description.
   c. Hand the answer sheet to the instructor for checking.

1. Unit	1. Marking procedure for correspondence to facilitate filing.
2. Storing	2. Preliminary alphabetizing of papers according to captions.
3. Sorting	3. Mental determination of caption under which correspondence will be filed.
4. Release marks	4. Each part of a name used in alphabetizing.
5. Label	5. Easily accessible filing cabinets for frequently used records.
6. Collecting	6. Titles printed on guide tabs.
7. Individual folder	7. Notations indicating correspondence is ready to be filed.
8. Indexing	8. The first step in preparing correspondence for the file.
9. Finding	9. Should be used to identify a folder.
10. Filing	10. Standard, vertical storage place for files.
11. Drawer	11. Has the basic function of storage and accessibility.

(continued on next page)

12. Coding
13. Classifying
14. Captions
15. Active files

Projects

Project 1. *A Case Study*

Purpose: This project aims to give you experience in

1. talking with people who work with filing systems
2. evaluating the standard filing practices described in this Chapter
3. drawing conclusions about some standard filing practices you observed in a business office.

Instructions:

1. With your instructor's approval, interview an employee who maintains a correspondence file for her employer.
2. Discuss with this employee the eight standard practices described in this Chapter.
3. Prepare a report for your instructor that describes practices this employee used that differ from those discussed in this Chapter. Find out (and report) *why* the employee used different practices.
4. To what degree do you think office employees should depart from textbook ideas they learned while in school? Why?
5. What filing practices did you learn about in the office you visited that have not been discussed yet in this Workbook?

4

Correspondence Filing Systems

Office correspondence files are usually handled by secretaries. The contents of such files represent a considerable dollar investment to a business; the cost of writing and mailing an average letter is estimated to be more than three dollars, and many letters cost more than that. Letters serve as pipelines to customers, the general public, suppliers, and co-workers in branch divisions. They are a primary way to communicate with people. Even when business is handled by telephone, people tend to say, "Put that in writing," "Send me a letter about it," and "Will you confirm this by letter, please?" An efficient correspondence file is, therefore, important to managers. Generally, managers depend on secretaries for expertise in organizing and handling the files.

Although correspondence files are usually straight alphabetical name systems, a secretary still has many things to consider when organizing and handling them. For example:

1. What kinds of guides and folders should she use?
2. What kind of an alphabetical breakdown should she use?
3. What kind of tab notations should she recommend? Open or closed?
4. How should she use color coding?
5. How should she arrange the guides and folders?

6. What kind of cabinets should she recommend? Two-drawer? Three-drawer? Four-drawer? Five-drawer?

7. Should she recommend a commercially prepared "system" or should she make up her own?

8. What allowances should she make for special guides and folders?

9. What should she do about correspondents who write almost daily so that their folders soon are full?

10. What should she do when the file drawers become overcrowded?

11. Where should the files be located in relation to her work station?

12. Should the boss take and return materials directly from and to the files? After all, they are *his* files.

13. How can she coordinate the correspondence files with other office filing systems such as catalogs, reports, and card files?

14. How can she keep old, seldom-used materials weeded out of the correspondence files?

There are other things to consider, too. For example, should she ask her boss to answer the questions we have just raised? If she is in charge of the files, how much authority should she have? How much responsibility should she take for the decisions? Since she and her boss work as a team, the ideal arrangement is for her to consult him about filing problems but, at the same time, since the files are her responsibility, she should be prepared to recommend solutions. This means that a secretary should know more about alphabetical name filing systems than just indexing rules and steps in the filing procedure. She needs to know about all the areas that are discussed in this chapter.

The File Folder[1]

Never place loose papers in a file drawer. All papers should go in identified folders. Ideally, a folder should be thin, stiff, and strong with a smooth surface finish so that it resists soiling and slides easily in and out of a file drawer. The protrusion at the edge of a folder is a *tab*. Tabs come in various widths and may be located in various posi-

---

[1] Chapter 5, Filing Supplies and Equipment, goes into more detail about guides, folders, cabinets, and other filing supplies and equipment.

tions along the folder's edge, or even along the side. The various types
of tab cuts are illustrated in Fig. 4–1. (These will be discussed more
fully later in this chapter.)

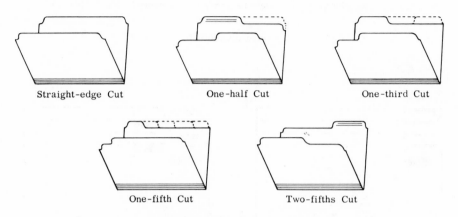

Straight-edge Cut   One-half Cut   One-third Cut

One-fifth Cut   Two-fifths Cut

Figure 4–1. Folder tab cuts

Folders are made of manila, kraft, jute, pressboard, or mibran
fiber. They are scored at the bottom so they can be expanded. Top-
grade folders come in different weights. For example, a top-grade
manila folder comes in 8-point (medium), 11-point (heavy), and 14-
point (extra heavy) weights.

A correspondence file uses *individual* name folders and *miscellaneous* folders. Papers are accumulated in miscellaneous folders until
there are five or six for the same name. At that time, if the correspondence is likely to continue active, an individual folder is made.

Miscellaneous Folders

A miscellaneous folder carries the same alphabetical caption as the
preceding guide. Sometimes it is placed directly behind the guide, but
more often it is placed behind the individual folders. Usually there is
one miscellaneous folder for each guide. A unique color may be used
for the captions of miscellaneous folders by using a colored label.
This makes the miscellaneous folder easier to locate. Assigning the
same tab position to all miscellaneous folders down the length of the
drawers also helps to locate them quickly.

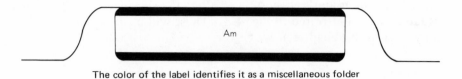

The color of the label identifies it as a miscellaneous folder

Figure 4-2. A miscellaneous folder tab

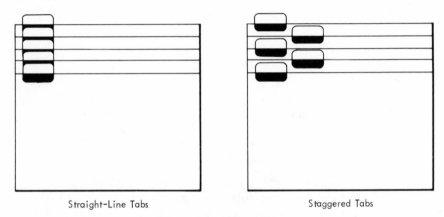

Straight-Line Tabs   Staggered Tabs

Figure 4-3. Tab positions

Since miscellaneous folders contain a variety of items, their contents must be organized. Contents are arranged alphabetically by name first; when there is more than one item for a name, these are arranged by date, with the most recent date to the front (on top).

Individual Folders

When a folder is made for an individual correspondent, the full name should be typed on a label which is then pasted over the tab. It is helpful if the first filing unit is underlined or capitalized. Sometimes the address or a cross reference is included on the label.

When an individual folder becomes crowded make another; (usually around 100 items is the maximum for one folder). The resulting series of folders for one individual may be coordinated by numbering the folders or, better yet, by showing the dates of the period covered. This information is typed on the tab.

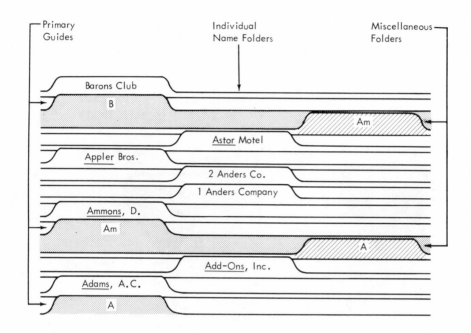

Figure 4-4. A correspondence filing system

In Fig. 4-4 all tabs are one-third cuts. Main guides are in the first position, individual folders in the first and second positions, and miscellaneous folders in the third position. Note that there are two folders for Anders Company. They are numbered to denote sequence; the range of dates each folder contains is not shown.

Guides

Guides are signposts in a file. They also help to keep folders upright and to prevent sagging. Stiff and strong pressboard guides are the most widely used kind, although celluloid- or plastic-coated ones are more soil resistant. For less active files, fiberboard or even lightweight manila guides may be used.

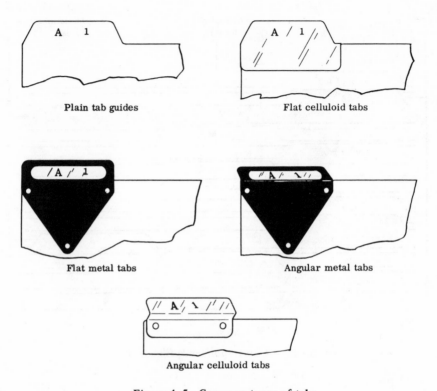

Figure 4-5. Common types of tabs

The tabs on guides also come in various widths and positions. (See Fig. 4-5.) Tabs are said to be in staggered positions when they occupy all positions from left to right in a file drawer.

Tabs

Staggered tabs are useful because several headings are visible at once. Many people, however, prefer straight-line arrangements. Third- or fifth-cut tabs are popular. A third-cut means that a tab occupies one-third of the space along the edge of a folder; a fifth-cut tab occupies one-fifth of the space. (See Fig. 4-1.)

Tabs may be of the reinforced type or they may be a mere extension of the back of a guide or folder. Some tabs are designed for insertable labels. On guides, tabs may be edged with metal and riveted to the guide. Such tabs are very durable. Black, rustproof enamel edgings are perhaps the most durable. Some tabs are angular and slant back for maximum visibility.

Preprinted tabs are available with alphabetic captions. The number of captions desired is a matter of study and preference and depends on the size of the file. The percentage of names beginning with each letter of the alphabet varies widely depending on the nature of the business and its geographic location. Generally, however, it has been estimated that 50 percent of all names begin with either *B, C, H, M, S,* or *W.*

Table 4-1 is based on a study made by the Navy Department of the distribution frequencies of about 7 million surnames. A similar study made by the Social Security Administration is also shown. The numbers in the table show the frequency with which last names start with each letter of the alphabet as determined by the two studies.

TABLE 4-1.
CLASSIFICATION DIVISION FREQUENCIES IN NAME FILES

Letter Category	Navy Frequency* (%)	SSA Frequency† (%)	Letter Category	Navy Frequency (%)	SSA Frequency (%)
A	3.15	(3.051)	De-Dh	1.24	
A-Ak	.72		Di-Dn	.63	
Al	.72		Do-Dt	1.17	
Am-Aq	.84		Du-Dz	.82	
Ar-Az	.87		E	1.94	(1.888)
B	9.46	(9.357)	E-Ek	.71	
B-Bd	2.06		El-Em	.45	
Be-Bh	1.61		En-Ez	.78	
Bi-Bk	.43		F	3.58	(3.622)
Bl-Bn	.46		F-Fd	.54	
Bo-Bq	1.11		Fe-Fh	.43	
Br-Bt	2.30		Fi-Fk	.57	
Bu-Bz	1.49		Fl-Fq	1.07	
C	7.40	(7.267)	Fr-Fz	.97	
C-Cg	2.07		G	4.92	(5.103)
Ch-Ck	1.04		G-Gd	1.04	
Cl-Cn	.68		Ge-Gh	.37	
Co-Cq	2.33		Gi-Gn	.85	
Cr-Ct	.78		Go-Gq	.86	
Cu-Cz	.50		Gr-Gz	1.80	
D	5.17	(4.783)			
D-Dd	1.31				

Better File Operations, Navy Management Office, Department of the Navy, Washington 25, D.C. (1957), pp. 27–28.

†Social Security Administration distribution of last names by initial letter. The SSA has also published a list of some 1,500 most common names arranged alphabetically by size.

TABLE 4-1 (continued)

Letter Category	Navy Frequency (%)	SSA Frequency (%)	Letter Category	Navy Frequency (%)	SSA Frequency (%)
H	7.74	(7.440)	Pe-Pg	1.19	
H-Hd	2.91		Ph	.26	
He-Hh	1.27		Pi-Pn	.62	
Hi-Hn	.79		Po-Pq	.77	
Ho-Ht	1.77		Pr-Pz	.74	
Hu-Hz	1.00		Q	.18	(.175)
I	.39	(.387)	R	5.14	(5.257)
J	2.84	(2.954)	R-Rd	.74	
J-Jd	.68		Re-Rh	1.02	
Je-Jn	.39		Ri-Rn	.90	
Jo-Jz	1.77		Ro-Rt	1.84	
K	3.91	(3.938)	Ru-Rz	.64	
K-Kd	.52		S	10.03	(10.194)
Ke-Kh	1.03		S-Sb	1.04	
Ki-Kn	1.25		Sc-Sd	1.31	
Ko-Kq	.46		Se-Sg	.52	
Kr-Kz	.65		Sh	1.09	
L	4.69	(4.664)	Si-Sl	1.03	
L-Ld	1.46		Sm	1.21	
Le-Lh	1.26		Sn-So	.50	
Li-Ln	.62		Sp-Ss	.54	
Lo-Lt	.79		St	1.97	
Lu-Lz	.56		Su-Sz	.82	
M	9.57	(9.448)	T	3.31	(3.450)
M-Mb	2.73		T-Tg	.93	
Mc-Md	2.30		Th-Tn	1.11	
Me-Mh	.74		To-Tq	.41	
Mi-Mn	1.30		Tr-Tz	.86	
Mo-Mt	1.65		U	.22	(.238)
Mu-Mz	.85		V	1.09	(1.279)
N	1.72	(1.785)	W	6.26	(6.287)
N-Nd	.24		W-Wd	1.61	
Ne-Nh	.67		We-Wg	1.00	
Ni-Nz	.81		Wh	.68	
O	1.43	(1.436)	Wi-Wn	1.96	
O-Ok	.47		Wo-Wz	1.01	
Ol-Oz	.96		X	(‡)	(.003)
P	4.90	(4.887)	Y	.49	(.555)
P-Pd	1.32		Z	.47	(.552)

‡Less than 0.005

The number of alphabetic guides used in a correspondence filing system is a matter of judgment based on how much is to be filed and how fast the file may expand. Alphabetic guides range from sets of 23 (*ij* and *xyz* combined) to sets of 250,000. Naturally, the 250,000 subdivision would be used only in a huge system. The most commonly used sets contain 40, 80, 120, 160, and 240 guides. The latter is suitable for a 10-drawer file.

Alphabetical classifications on tabs may be either single or double. Double classifications (Ca-Cm) are also known as closed captions. Single captions are preferred if a filing system is expanding because one cannot insert a Cc-Cf caption if the system already contains a Ca-Cm guide. However, there are those who prefer double captions because they show clearly the starting and closing letters of the section. Individual folders filed behind a guide have names that begin with the first classification printed on the tab and go through the second classification. Hence, file behind the closed caption Ca-Cm, names that begin with *Ca, Cb, Cc, Cd, Ce, Cf, Cg, Ch, Ci, Cj, Ck, Cl,* and *Cm. Cn* would be filed behind the *next* guide.

Labels

Insertable labels are best for heavy wear. Files are neater if the labels are typewritten. When labels contain several lines, type them in blocked form. This also contributes to neatness. Labels come individually or in strips (see Figs. 4–6 and 4–7). Color may be used to code certain types of guides or folders. Color-coding miscellaneous folders has already been discussed.

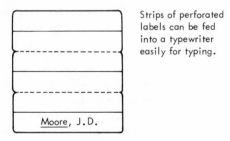

Strips of perforated labels can be fed into a typewriter easily for typing.

Moore, J.D.

Figure 4–6. A strip of labels

Guide and Folder Systems

Systematizing the position of guide tabs is a first step in organizing a successful file. Uniformity in the arrangement speeds up both filing and finding. An example of a systematized arrangement for guide tabs is illustrated in Fig. 4–8. (See also Fig. 4–4.)

Figure 4–7. A continuous feed of box labels
(courtesy Oxford Pendaflex Corp.)

In the system shown in Fig. 4–8, the primary guides are in the first two positions in a one-fifth cut. Because this system used a type of closed caption with the captions numbered; expansion is restricted. The miscellaneous folders, one-fifth cut, are in the third position and are located just ahead of the next primary guide. The primary guides have durable metal edged tabs into which caption labels may be inserted. For this reason, guides will not be lost when the system is ex-

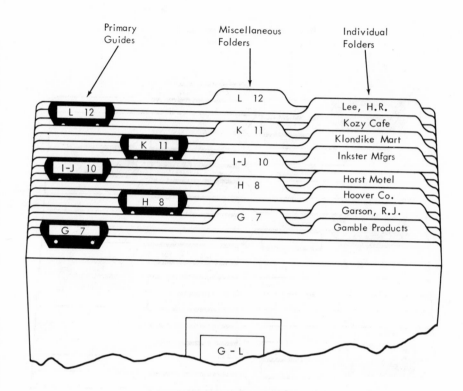

Figure 4-8. An alphabetic file

panded. New inserts must, however, be prepared for all of them. The individual folders are a two-fifths cut in the last position.

Most filing equipment and supply manufacturers have developed so-called standardized systems. They usually will be glad to send a representative to your office to consult about designing a system for your needs. (See the list of filing equipment and supply companies in the Appendix of this Workbook.)

A question secretaries and their bosses often ask is, "Should we use a commercially arranged, standard system?" A well-known one is Remington Rand's Variadex System, which is illustrated in Fig. 4-9. Fig. 4-10 shows Globe-Wernicke's Safeguard System.

The Variadex system color codes alphabetic subdivisions, as described in Fig. 4-9. The idea is that color can be identified almost instantly and speeds up filing. Another Remington Rand system,

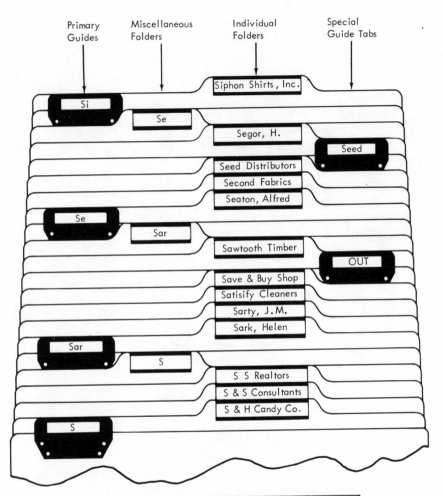

If the 2nd letter of the 1st unit of the name is:	The color on the guide & folder tabs for that section will be:
a, b, c, d	Orange
e, f, g, h	Yellow
i, j, k, l, m, n	Green
o, p, q	Blue
r, s, t, u, v, w, x, y, z,	Violet

Figure 4-9. Variadex filing system
(*courtesy Remington Rand Office Systems*)

Triplecheck, uses numbers as well as letters and colors, on the tabs. Table 4–2 names other standard systems and their manufacturers and describes some of their features.

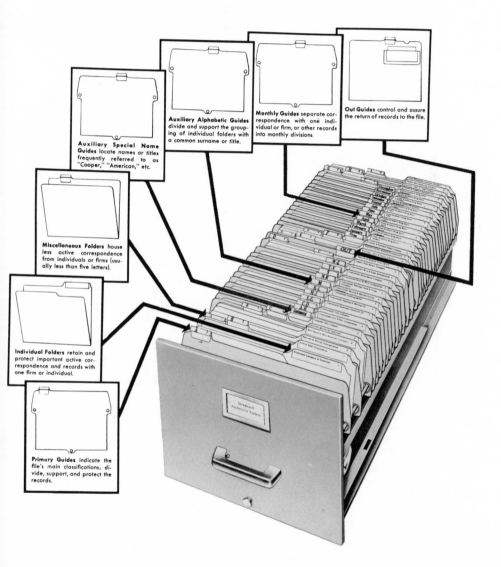

Figure 4–10. The "Safeguard" alphabetic system
(*courtesy Globe-Wernicke Co.*)

TABLE 4-2. STANDARD FILING SYSTEMS

System	No. of Positions	First Position	Second Position	Third Position	Fourth Position	Fifth Position	Color?	Numeric?
Amfile or Amberg-Nual (Amberg File and Index Co.) 1627 Duane Blvd. Kankakee, Ill. 60901	4	Special guides Miscellaneous folders in front of individual folders	Alphabetic guides Individual folders ——Staggered—→	Alphabetic guides	Alphabetic guides Individual folders ——→	None	No	Primary guides numbered consecutively; everything following primary guide bears same number
Safeguard Alphabetic Index (Globe-Wernicke) 1505 Jefferson Toledo, Ohio 43624	5	Alphabetic guides numbered Miscellaneous folders	Alphabetic guides numbered Miscellaneous folders ——Staggered—→	Alphabetic guides numbered Miscellaneous folders	Special guides	Individual folders	Guides green Miscellaneous folders red Individual folders red or orange	Primary guides numbered consecutively
Super Index Ideal (Shaw-Walker) 1950 Townsend St. Muskegon, Mich. 49443	4	Alphabetic guides numbered ——Staggered—→ Miscellaneous folders	Alphabetic guides numbered ——Staggered—→	Individual folders —— Staggered —→ Out guides	Individual folders Special guides	None	None	Primary guides numbered consecutively
Tel-I-Vision (Smead Mfg. Co.) 309 Second St. Hastings, Minn. 55033	4	Alphabetic guides numbered ——Staggered—→	Alphabetic guides numbered ——Staggered—→	Miscellaneous folders	Individual folders with wide tabs extending across both positions	None	Miscellaneous folders green	Primary guides numbered consecutively; everything following primary guide bears same number
Triple Check Automatic (Remington-Rand Office Systems) Box 171 Marietta, Ohio 45750	5	White guides covering alphabet A = 10 B = 20 C = 30 etc.	Guides with 9 sections of alphabet color coded	Miscellaneous folders	Individual folders	Special name guides Out guides	3 colors in alphabetic guides for second breakdown	Numbers assigned to each folder by location in alphabet
Variadex (Remington-Rand)	4	Alphabetic guides	Miscellaneous folders	Individual folders	Special name guides	None	Guide and folder tabs colored in rainbow sequence; all folders same color as their primary guide	

In spite of differences among systems in arranging locations of tabs for guides, folders, and special situations, the basic function of all alphabetical name filing systems is the same. Each collects papers in folders that are sequenced behind guides. Each has miscellaneous as well as individual folders. Each may include special guides or folders. Within the individual folders items may be arranged by date.

Filing Cabinets

Correspondence filing cabinets are manufactured in various sizes. There are two-, three-, four-, and even five-drawer cabinets. Their body structure varies in that some are highly insulated whereas others are merely tin boxes. Some have combination locks on drawers, others use keys. A four-drawer cabinet is shown in Fig. 4-11.

Figure 4-11. A four-drawer filing cabinet
(*courtesy Meilink Steel Safe Co.*)

Correspondence filing cabinets are often referred to as vertical files because items stand on edge in the file drawers. The drawers themselves range from 20 to 28 inches deep and from 12 to 22 inches wide. They can handle letter, legal, or longer papers and documents.

The standard drawer used for correspondence files is 26 inches deep and can hold about 4,000 pieces of paper, including folders and guides. Usually, about twenty to twenty-five guides are used in a drawer. Not more than ten folders should go behind a guide. More than 4,000 sheets can be put into a drawer, but then there would not be enough working space. Five inches of working space is needed in a file drawer *after* the follow block has been pushed back. Crowded files are hard to work in and cause torn contents and filing errors.

Drawers are labeled to identify contents. These labels are often color coded.

Open file drawers are an accident hazard in an office, causing cuts and bruises. Furthermore, filing cabinets may become top-heavy and fall forward if top drawers are left open. For these reasons, anyone working with files should be careful. Close a file drawer immediately after you have finished working in it.

Soundex

If one carefully and consistently follows a good set of alphabetizing rules for indexing names, it is fairly easy to maintain a well-organized system. But the exact spelling of a name cannot always be established, or the file may contain names that are pronounced the same but spelled differently; for example, Nickels, Nickells, Nickolas, etc.

Two things can be done in this case: (1) names may be grouped under one common spelling and cross referenced; or (2) names may be filed by phonetic spelling (Soundex) rather than letter by letter. When a system is large and contains many similar sounding words or foreign or unusual names with difficult spellings, a phonetic system may be helpful. The authors have seen this system used very effectively in a large medical center, where delays in finding medical records because of the spelling of a name can be a matter of life or death, especially when the victim has been in an accident and there is a great deal of confusion.

A Soundex system phonetically groups names that sound alike regardless of spelling. Spelling subtleties such as *ie* and *ei* and double consonants are disregarded. Phonetic filing is obtained by dropping vowels (Jcbs for Jacobs, Jcbsn for Jacobson) and by grouping and coding similar-sounding consonants. For example:

1. BFPV   4. L
2. CGJKQSXZ   5. MN
3. DT   6. R

To code for Soundex, the initial letter of the name is retained as spelled: *w* and *h* are dropped entirely except as initial letters. Double consonants (or equivalent letters) are coded as one letter unless separated by a vowel or a *y*, which are otherwise disregarded within a name. After the initial letter, a name is coded up to three characters. Zeros are added when necessary to complete three digits. For example:

Sinclair	S524	Lowery	L600	Sachs	S220
St. Clair	S530	Laughrey	L260	Saxe	S200

The "sound" system described above is a well-known one and was originally developed by the Remington Rand Corporation's American Filing Bureau. The system was first known as the Russell Soundex System. Today there are many variations of it because of the personal preferences of those working with it and because, as the names shown illustrate, it is not entirely dependable. It sometimes groups unrelated or dissimilar names such as Hall and Howeley and does not group such similar names as those used in the preceding example.

Review Questions

1. What kinds of things should a secretary know about alphabetic correspondence filing systems in addition to the indexing rules and filing procedures?
2. What do you consider when selecting a file folder for a correspondence system?
3. What do you consider when selecting a guide?
4. What is a miscellaneous folder? Why are they necessary in a correspondence system?
5. How is color coding used in correspondence filing systems?
6. What is meant by the term "cut" when referring to file folders and guides?
7. What are single-caption tabs? Double-caption tabs?
8. What is an advantage of a double-caption tab? Of a single-caption tab?
9. How many papers should an individual folder hold? How few?
10. Why use labels on tabs in filing? Which is better; the paste-on or the window insert? What are the advantages of each?

11. What is the basic function of all correspondence filing systems?
12. Why have so many "standardized" systems been prepared by manufacturers?
13. What function do guides have in a correspondence filing system?
14. How should folders and guides be arranged in a file drawer?
15. To what extent can a secretary be innovative in designing a correspondence filing system?
16. What are some features of standardized filing systems?
17. How many papers does a file drawer usually hold?
18. Why is working space necessary in a file drawer?
19. How is a follow block used in a file drawer?
20. How does one decide what sort of alphabetical breakdown to use?
21. What part should the boss have in setting up and maintaining an alphabetic filing system?
22. What is "Soundex" filing? Where is it used?

Review Exercises

Review Exercise 1

Draw an outline of an alphabetical correspondence filing system similar to the ones shown in this chapter. Show where primary guides, miscellaneous folders, and individual folders will be located. Describe how you would use color in the system. Print in the captions and appropriate names on individual folder tabs. Which will you use, open or closed captions? Remember, the Remington-Rand Triple Check system also uses color coding. It uses numbers, letters, *and* colors.

Review Exercise 2

Use the text or a dictionary for definitions of the following words and terms. Type them and hand them to the teacher for checking.

1. Caption	6. Drawer file
2. Label	7. Documents
3. Tab	8. Follow block
4. Straight-line file	9. Kraft
5. Alphabetic breakdowns	10. Manila

Review Exercise 3. Soundex Filing

Using the phonetic filing system described in the text, indicate the code number for each of the following names:

a.	Behr, Baier, Bayer	f.	Cline, Klein
b.	McElroy, McIlroy	g.	Philbrick, Filbrick
c.	Niccollai, Nickolay	h.	Ebel, Able
d.	Canady, Kennedy	i.	McCrea, McRea
e.	Wray, Ray	j.	Weinberg, Wineberg

On the basis of this project, what are some of the conclusions you reach about phonetic filing?

Project 1. *A Capsule Case*

Purpose: This project aims to give you experience in

1. analyzing a case in which a correspondence file needs to be separated from, yet coordinated with, a file of technical information;
2. discussing with your classmates and instructor the *pros* and *cons* of possible solutions for this capsule case.

The Case: The Technical Information Department of Stanton Chemical Corporation has been systematically collecting, indexing, and storing technical information and related correspondence about various chemicals in an alphabetical file for more than twenty years. Recently, because of some new developments, this information has become very active, and the twenty-year accumulation of records has become voluminous. Although some information has historical value, some of it no longer has immediate, practical value.

In an effort to cut down on the sheer quantity of records that have to be fingered and searched when a retrieval is to be made, management has asked the Technical Information Department to separate the correspondence from the report forms, tabulations of data, and clippings and library reference recapitulations. (No items are larger than 8½ by 11″.) The two types of records, although separated, are to be coordinated so that related information from either file can be retrieved with a minimum of searching. The primary emphasis, however, is to be on a system that will make it possible to retrieve the technical information first in order to answer immediate questions, and also as a resource from which to draw data for a new technical publication the Corporation is starting.

Instructions: Prepare a short, neatly typewritten report for your employer outlining suggestions for the following aspects of the above case problem:

1. A correspondence file that will systematically batch and organize the twenty-year accumulation of correspondence. Keep in mind retrieval and accurate coordination with related records.
2. A coordinating index for about 85 carefully selected vocabulary terms developed by the Corporation's laboratories for identifying specific items in both the correspondence and technical data files. (A coordinating index has not been discussed yet in this workbook. This is your chance to do some creative thinking about how such a coordinating index might work to bridge the gap between these two separate, yet related, sets of records.)
3. Write five questions that need to be asked in analyzing the above case. Preferably they should not be questions that are answered by a mere "yes" or "no."

Note. The above case is an exercise in analysis; there are no specific correct answers. *Why* is an important question to raise throughout the analysis. That is, when a recommendation is made, examine it from the point of view of *why* it might or might not be practical or feasible.

5

Filing Supplies and Equipment

When setting up a filing system, it is desirable to choose suitable supplies and equipment because they are an important part of a filing system. However, there are so many different kinds to choose from that it is often hard to decide which to use. (See Appendix C, Filing Equipment and Supply Companies.) Once a decision has been made, though, supplies and equipment should be standardized as much as possible. Standardization simplifies buying, keeps systems uniform and neater, and makes integration among filing systems easier.

Types of Filing Equipment

Various types of filing equipment are discussed here: (1) Drawer files, (2) Shelf files, and (3) Special items such as folders, guides and signals. It is impossible in a Workbook of this size to include information about all of the types of equipment manufactured in these categories, so the following is merely introductory, and trade names of specific products or names of manufacturers are not used.

1. Drawer Files

Drawer files are 24, 26, or 28 inches deep. A standard 26-inch drawer holds 3500–5000 sheets in addition to the necessary guides and folders. Drawers vary in width from letter (12½ inches) to legal size (15½ inches). Most file drawers are 10 3/8 inches high. A file folder is 9 inches high plus a ½ inch tab so there is a 7/8 inch clearance (10 3/8 – 9½ at top of the drawer). Even with metal-tabbed guides the folders measure no higher than 10 inches so there is 3/8 of an inch in the clear with the tallest supplies.

Four-drawer files are commonly used, although three-drawer files serve the added purpose of providing a counter over which to serve the public. One- and two-drawer files are sometimes used as desk files. Five- and six-drawer files also are available and have the advantage of conserving space. An increasing number of them are being used in offices; however, they are not recommended for active files.

Interchangeability of file drawers is a feature that influences the usefulness of the equipment. As the contents of a drawer become less active, they should be moved to a low-priority location, and it is easier to transfer the entire drawer than to unload and then reload the contents. Thus interchangeable drawers provide flexibility within a filing system.

Quality Features. Several features distinguish a top quality drawer file. These drawers have special mechanical features. For example, when a drawer is filled with papers, it weighs between 60 and 70 pounds. To prevent loaded drawers from sliding out of the cabinet when they are open, they should move on telescoping slides that move on ball bearing rollers. (See Fig. 5-1.) Files with insulated walls that can withstand intense heat from fire may be necessary for vital records. Since they cost more than ordinary files, their use should be limited to cases where fireproofing is an important criterion.

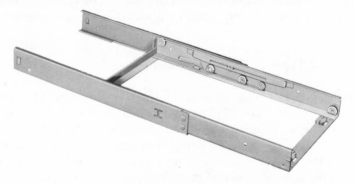

Figure 5-1. Telescoping slides support drawers
(*courtesy Datavue Products Corp.*)

File drawers should also be braced for rigidity, since the weight of contents can cause a drawer to sag. (See Fig. 5-2.) Another quality feature is a guide rod that runs through holes in the middle of the bottom of each guide and holds it in place while the file is being used.

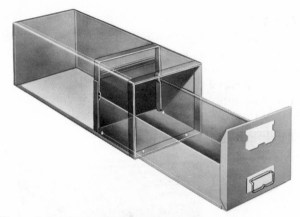

Figure 5-2. Cutaway of a drawer showing reinforced frame
(*courtesy Diebold, Inc.*)

Security Locks. A desirable feature for a file is a security lock. Gang locks lock and unlock all drawers in one operation. Other types include those with a combination lock on one drawer of a three- or four-drawer cabinet. (See Fig. 5-3.)

Figure 5-3. A four-drawer file cabinet with a combination lock
(*courtesy Diebold, Inc.*)

Follow Block. Until a file drawer is full, some device is needed to hold the folders upright. A common supplement in a file drawer for this purpose is a *follow block* or *compressor.* This device should slide back and forth easily on its guide rails at the bottom of the drawer and lock into the desired position automatically.

Innovation. Any innovations in drawer files that save space are important. Files with drop-fronts provide four extra inches of working space when pulled forward. (See Fig. 5–4.)

Figure 5–4. File with drop front provides extra working space
(*courtesy The General Fireproofing Co.*)

Another space-saving idea is to reduce the dimensions of the file cabinet itself. By making the drawers shallower, a six-drawer cabinet uses the same area as a conventional five-drawer file. It allows only 11/16 of an inch for tab clearance in a drawer.

An innovation in drawer filing is lateral placement guides. Manufacturers claim that this arrangement provides 21 percent more filing capacity. (See Fig. 5–5.)

Figure 5-5. Lateral Pendaflexer file cabinets save space
(courtesy Oxford Pendaflex Corp.)

Suspension or "hanging" files has been widely adopted as an improvement over conventional files. In this system, folders and guides hang on an inner drawer frame so that they do not rest on the bottom of the drawer where they sometimes slump and sag. Some of the disadvantages of suspension files are that they use extra space in a drawer, that the initial cost of frames and folders is greater, and unless regular folders are placed inside them, they are less convenient to use outside the files. They are also costly and slightly inconvenient to use in inactive storage. (See Fig. 5-6.)

A distinctive feature of one type of popular suspension file is that the tab is on the *front* half of the folder so that it is not obscured when you work in it. Also, if a signal or a wide tab is attached to the back of the folder with month and/or date markings, the folder becomes a follow-up file as well. Since a front-tabbed suspension folder becomes its own guide, the need for bulky, heavy metal-tabbed guides is eliminated.

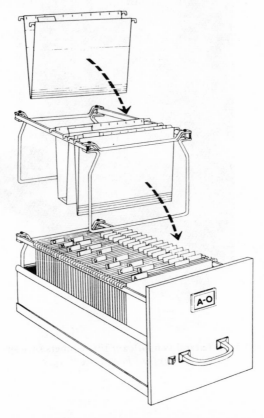

Figure 5-6. Pendaflex folder, frame, and folder attached to frame
(*courtesy Oxford Pendaflex Corp.*)

Special Equipment. Some records cause special housing problems. For example, how can offset mats, stencils, drawings, or blueprints be filed? The type of equipment available varies; in one system such items can be suspended on hangers (See Fig. 5-7). Blueprints and drawings can also be rolled and stored in a cabinet of tubes that resembles a honey-comb. An index to help locate the items is mounted on the door. Of course, blueprints and drawings can also be stored in flat drawers.

Figure 5-7. Stencil filed on removable hangers
(courtesy Gestetner Corp.)

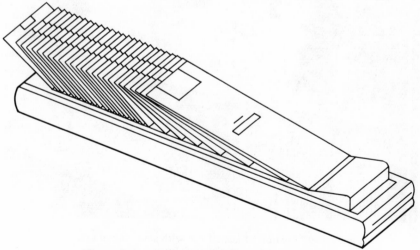

Figure 5-8. Sliding racks cut rough-sorting time
(courtesy National Archives and Records Service)

Sorters. Sorting devices provide captions for classifying papers by numbers or by alphabet. There are two main types: the 20-inch base for use on tables and the smaller 12-inch base for desk use. (See Fig. 5-8.)

2. Shelf Files

There is a trend to file materials on shelves rather than in drawers because folders are easier to get when filed in this way. (See Fig. 5-9.) Top-tabbed or side-tabbed folders may be used for shelf filing, but the guides must be side tabbed.

Ordinary folders like those used in drawer files may be transferred to shelf files. Dividers are used on shelf files to keep materials up-

**Figure 5-9. Portion of a shelf file with side-tabbed guides
and top-tabbed folders**
(courtesy Tab Products Co.)

right. The dividers may be portable paper or metal boxes, or movable single, metal sheets that hook into the file. (See Figs. 5–10 and 5–11.) A secretary who would probably use shelf files as a readily accessible supplementary filing area within arm's reach of her work station would no doubt use the portable boxes as dividers.

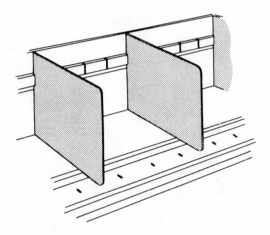

Figure 5–10. Metal sheet dividers

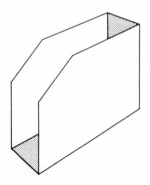

Figure 5–11. Portable box dividers

Figure 5-12. Files, two deep, arranged in tiers — the inner file rolls out;
the outer file moves laterally
(*courtesy Supreme Equipment and Systems*)

Folders

Seven factors influence the choice of file folders: (1) composition,
(2) finish, (3) size, (4) expansibility, (5) cut, (6) reinforcement, and
(7) tabs.

1. Composition

Folders are made of manila, kraft, pressboard, or patented composition such as *durox* or *dura-file*. A buyer may test a folder for
tensile strength by tearing it. This is how the government makes
durability tests.

Handwriting and typing on light colored manila folders are easy to
see, but some people prefer darker kraft because it does not soil

easily. Manila and kraft folders are used for everyday filing operations. Pressboard and the patented compositions are used for heavy-
duty files. Folders of different compositions may be used in the same
files.

The weight of a folder depends on the thickness of the material
of which it is made. This is gauged by a point system, a *point* being
1/1000 of an inch. The folder used in many companies is 11 points
(.011 inches), kraft composition. A 14-point super-stock kraft or
manila folder is recommended for heavily loaded and busy folders.
Pressboard or durox folders are recommended for unusual situations,
especially when drawer space is not a problem.

2. Finish

The finish on folders is the result of the *sizing* (a filler) used to give
body to paper from which the folders are made. In this way the
paper is hardened and folders are stiffened. Hard-finish folders wear
well.

3. Size

Correspondence-size folders are 11¾ inches wide; legal-size folders
are 15 inches wide.

4. Expansibility

Expansion folders of all sorts may be purchased. Folders expand
from less than an inch to 2 inches and more. Those with the greatest
expansion have cloth glued across their bottoms. These are suitable
for heavy loads of materials such as catalogs. Expansion files also
come in bellows styles that fan out when opened. (See Fig. 5–13.)

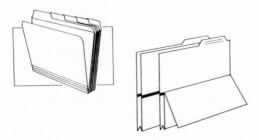

Figure 5–13. File pockets

Regular folders are *scored* across the front bottom, usually three times. An unscored folder cannot be expanded at the bottom so the contents tend to ride up in the folder when additional papers are added. Scored folders, on the other hand, can be creased at the bottom as papers are added, thus providing a flat bottom. New folds can be made along the second and third scores as needed. (See Fig. 5–14.)

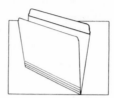

Figure 5-14. Tab-cut, reinforced, scored folder

When it is desirable to subdivide papers inside a folder, it is possible to buy folders with transparent plastic pockets, side pockets, and divider sheets (some with tabs). Bellows files also serve this purpose.

One type of file folder usually used for carrying papers rather than storing them is made of extremely durable red-rope paper and has a wide expansion capacity. It ordinarily has a flap and an attached reinforced tape or heavy elastic cord to hold down the flap, thus creating a secure carrying case. This type of folder wears well and is frequently used as a light briefcase. (See Fig. 5–15.)

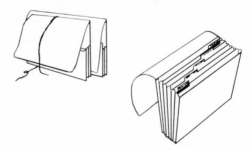

Figure 5-15. An expansible folder with a string may contain pockets

Binder Folders. When records are frequently used away from the files, they may be fastened to the inside of the folder with clamps. Folders with clamps in any of nine positions may be purchased. (See Fig. 5–16.) When binder folders are used extensively in a file, it is best to alternate the location of the clamps. Otherwise, they create an awkward bulge in the drawer at the point where the clamp is located.

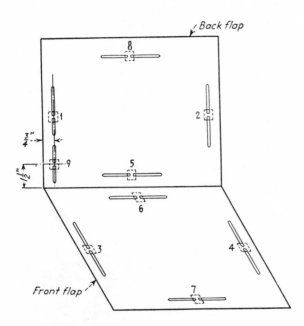

Figure 5-16. Location of fasteners in folders

5. Cut

Folder corners may be either square or rounded. Round corners do not become dog-eared as quickly as the square ones.

6. Reinforcement

Some folders are reinforced along the top edge, along the tab, or both. Reinforced folders are self-edged by folding over and gluing down the edge of the folder itself. The edge of a folder may also be covered with celluloid or a transparent synthetic to give it additional strength.

7. Tabs

The protrusion generally at the top of the back of a folder is the tab; the folder caption is placed there. The caption may be typed or written directly on the tab or on a label which is then glued over the tab. Captions for folders that are part of a commercial, patented filing system are usually preprinted.

   Tabs may be reinforced with celluloid, acetate, or a laminating
synthetic. If pressboard or heavy-duty folders are used, the tab frame
may be made of metal.
   Folders may be top-tabbed for use in drawer files, or side-tabbed
for shelf filing systems. Tabs for shelf-file folders extend beyond the
right-hand side of the back leaf of the folder and may be cut in
different styles. (See Fig. 5–17.)

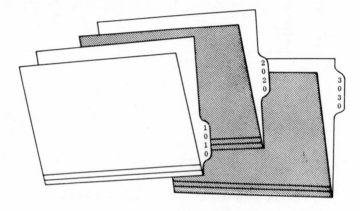

Figure 5–17. Side-tabbed folders

Guides

   As the name suggests, a *guide* directs the eye to the item wanted.
Main considerations in selecting guides are (1) composition and (2)
tabs. An additional feature is a reinforced hole at the bottom that
makes it possible to lock in and hold the guide on a rod inserted along
the bottom of the drawer.

1. Composition

   A 25-point (.025 inch) pressboard guide is recommended for
average use. Made of pressed wood pulp that has been highly surface-
sized, these guides are flexible without breaking and do not easily become dog-eared. A 20-point manila (wood sulphite) guide is suitable
for a temporary or transfer file. Aluminum guide frames are also
available. They have the advantage of adjustable tabs that may be
moved to any position desired.

2. Tabs

Tabs are even more important on guides than on folders. There are at least five types.

Plain tab guides may be purchased with blank or indexed tabs. Made of manila or pressboard, they are the least expensive tabs of all.

Flat celluloid tabs provide reinforcement and also serve to protect handwritten or printed labels.

Flat metal tabs have large openings into which removable insert labels may be slipped. These may be covered by colored, celluloid inserts that can be used both for protection and color control.

Angular metal tabs are tilted to a 45-degree angle so that they may be read easily at a distance. Magnified captions are also possible.

Angular celluloid tabs are also tilted at a 45-degree angle. These captions may also be magnified.

Signals

In addition to tabs that come permanently attached to guides and folders, it is possible to buy separate tabs that may be attached to them. These may be celluloid, acetate, laminated, or metal; straight, angled, or magnified. Strips of plastic tabs that may be cut to the desired size for attachment are also available. Detachable signal tabs usually fasten to the edge of a folder. Consider two guidelines when buying them: (1) They should "stay put," in the sense that they will not tend to move or get lost in the file; and (2) they should be thin enough so as not to add bulk to the files.

Alphabetic, monthly, weekly, and daily guide sets for follow-up files are available with various types of tabs. Weekly guides (seven, one for each day of the week) may be used behind monthly guides or (thirty-one, one for each day of the month).

Shelf-File Guides

Guides for shelf files are side-tabbed. The space for the captions is sometimes as long as 3½ inches. A debatable point about side-tabbed guides is whether they should read down or up. Most read down. (See Figs. 5–18 and 5–19.) Nearly all shelf-file manufacturers recommend that shelf-guide captions be in a uniform position (not staggered). The center position on a 9-inch guide is used most frequently.

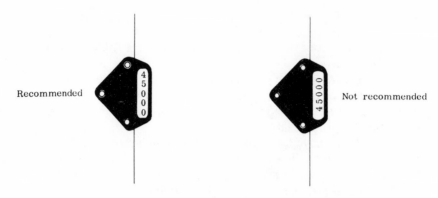

Figure 5-18.
Side-tabbed guides —
reading down

Figure 5-19.
Side-tabbed guides —
reading from the side

Most shelf-file guides have a sturdy metal hook projected from the back (see Fig. 5-20), which may be hooked to the back of the shelf so that it will not work forward on the shelf. The guide must be unhooked to be removed.

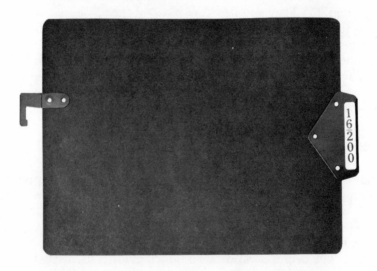

Figure 5-20. A hook-type projection lock on the guide
(*courtesy Datavue Products Corp.*)

Out Guides

Heavy manila out guides are top-tabbed for drawer filing systems and side-tabbed for shelf files. On the tab is a prominent caption that says OUT. One type of out guide has a celluloid pocket into which a memo form showing the name of the borrower and the date the item was borrowed may be inserted. There are also special types of out guides, such as substitution cards or colored sheets (with the OUT tab) to insert into folders. (See Fig. 5-21). Sometimes these are ruled for hand-entries to show the date the item was taken and who took it. Where entire files are removed, a specially designed out folder may be used. Here again, the front of the folder may be ruled so that "out" reference data may be recorded. Out folders are useful when papers are likely to be filed while the file itself is out. Loose papers (not in folders) should never be put into files.

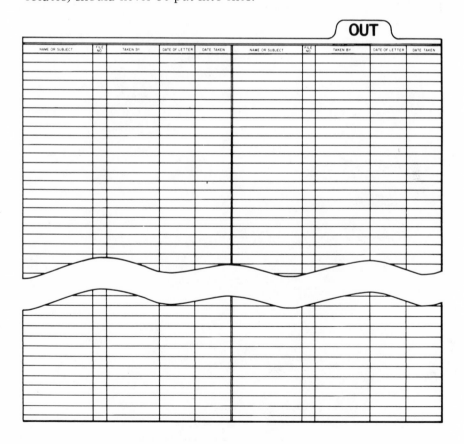

Figure 5-21. Out guide

Cross-Reference Sheets

Printed cross-reference sheets may be purchased, although it is a simple matter to duplicate them. A sample form is shown in Fig. 5–22.

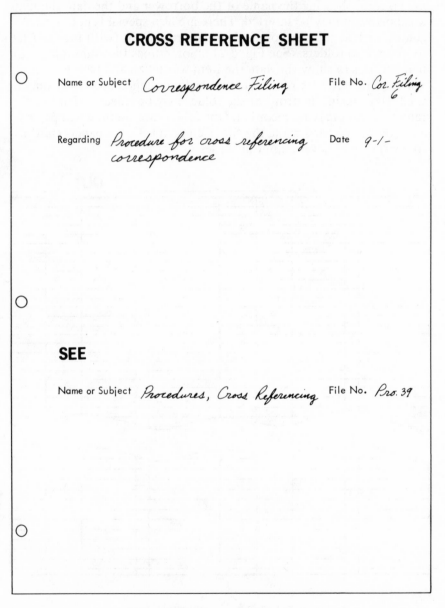

Figure 5–22. Cross-reference sheet

Review Questions

1. Why should an office employee who works with files know something about filing supplies and equipment?
2. Name some things to consider when selecting a drawer file.
3. What are the advantages of "hanging" folders?
4. Why are folders scored?
5. What are folder signals? How are they used?
6. What is the "weight" of a folder?
7. What is the "finish" of a folder?
8. What is the "composition" of a folder?
9. What is a bellows file? When is it used?
10. When should open-shelf filing be used?
11. What is an advantage of open-shelf filing? A disadvantage?
12. How are folders reinforced?
13. Describe a heavy-duty folder that might be used to file some bound catalogs.
14. Describe two types of out guides.
15. Describe a cross-reference sheet.
16. What is the capacity of an average file drawer?
17. What is a follow block?
18. What are some special features of a quality drawer file?
19. How can blueprints be filed?
20. How are sorters used?

Review Exercises

Review Exercise 1

a. Find dictionary definitions for the following terms.
b. Type the definitions neatly and hand them to your instructor for checking.

1. Compressor
2. Divider
3. Follow block
4. Position (1st, 2nd, etc.)
5. Suspension file (no-sag file)
6. Binder
7. Scoring
8. Sizing

Review Exercise 2

    a. File the names in each of the following groups in proper
       alphabetical order.
    b. Jot down the indexing rules that apply for each group.
    c. Prepare a suitable answer sheet and hand it to your
       instructor.

1. Charles R. Johnson
   Charles Johnson
   C. Johnson
   C. R. Johnson
   Charles David Johnson
   Carl Johnsen
2. Carlos de Constella
   Evetta d'Contas
   David Van Carlton
   Paul Van der Cortes
   Carl Vincent Compton
   Carlotta Consuela
     St. Charles
3. Benjamin Smith Health
     Center
   Smith-Borden Manufac-
     turing
   Survey Research Center
   Darold Smith
   Darwood-Smith Survey
     Company
   Betty Doris Smith
     (Mrs. Darold)
4. Natl Assoc. of Journalists
   Assoc. of Systems An-
     alysts
   Nation of World Fellow-
     ship
   Albert Ingers
   Al Ingers
   N.A.T.O.
5. Association of Personnel
     Officers

Association for Commu-
nity Welfare
Patterns in Living, Inc.
Committee of Financial
Advisors
Committee for Financial
Analysis
Association for Analysis
6. Los Angeles Mfg. Co.
Los Alamos Research
Center
Oregon City Transfer
Service
Oregon Tourist Service
North Dakota Printing
Co.
North Carolina Adoption
Center
7. Vandines Novelties, Inc.
Vance Newman
Vita Home for Children
View Lodge
View and Vie Shoppers
Nancy Vincent
8. 40 Club
Sixty St. Bookshop
The 12th St. Shop
The 2-Spot Meat Market
Twain and Fort, Attys.
The Four Winds
9. Natl Bank & Trust Co.,
San Francisco
Federal Savings & Loan
Co., San Francisco
Marine Trust Co. of Los
Angeles, Calif.
First Natl. Bank of Port-
land, Oregon
United States Bank of
Portland, Oregon
Natl City Bank of San
Diego, Calif.

Project 1. *Supply Research*

Purpose: This project aims to:
   a. help you learn about filing supplies and equipment;
   b. become acquainted with names of suppliers, both local and national;
   c. motivate you to use the list of suppliers in the Appendix;
   d. organize a folder of reference materials.

Project Materials:

   1. Pictures, clippings, brochures, and drawings of filing supplies and equipment.
   2. A folder.
   3. An index or table of contents that classifies and organizes the materials. (Made by the student.)

Instructions:

   1. Consult the list of filing suppliers in the Appendix.
   2. Check magazines and newspapers for pictures and advertisements of filing supplies and equipment.
   3. Focus on *one* type of supply or equipment: drawer cabinets, folders, tabs, or something new that was not discussed in this chapter. We recommend not getting into computer equipment because your project may get too complex. Files for computer tapes or disks would be all right though.
   4. If your instructor approves, visit a local office supply company or write to four or five of the file companies and ask for illustrative literature.
   5. Cut and mount on sheets of stationery at least *10* illustrations of the type of filing supply or equipment you chose to specialize in.
   6. Prepare an organized index or table of contents for the materials. (Be sure to note trade names, names of manufacturers, and model numbers.)
   7. Hand the project to the instructor. (Suggest to the instructor that some of the projects might be used on the bulletin board.)

6

Subject Filing Systems

The yellow pages of a telephone book are an example of subject filing. A telephone directory is also a good example of how we complement an alphabetic name file with a subject file. Can you imagine trying to find the name and telephone number of a television repairman in your neighborhood, of a pet hospital, or of a used car dealer without the yellow pages? You couldn't do it unless you knew the names of individuals in these businesses.

Businesses use subject filing for the following reasons:

1. To expand individual name correspondence files.
2. To organize papers that can be called for by subject as well as by individual names.
3. To group together in one folder papers about a single topic such as *Unions* or *Office Supplies.*
4. To organize records that fall into several classifications or subdivisions. (See Section 2 of this chapter: Encyclopedic Arrangement for Subject Files.)

As a business correspondence filing system grows, the need soon arises for subject classifications. (Subject classifications are also referred to as topics, headings, captions, titles, or descriptors.) Subjects such as *applications, tax records, insurance records,* and *speaking dates* are found in even the smallest correspondence filing systems. Often correspondence with companies involves both names of individuals and subject classifications; for example, a letter might be from Mr. Channing E. Gregory, president of D. C. Lloyd and Company, who is also chairman of the community's Red Feather Drive. The letter is written on D. C. Lloyd and Company letterhead but it is about the Red Feather Drive. The addressee has the choice of filing the letter under Mr. Gregory's name (where he will be able to find it only if he remembers that Mr. Gregory is this year's Drive chairman), or under some topic that he can recall easily. Probably the correspondence would be filed in a subject folder and cross referenced to Mr. Gregory's name. Subject topics under which this correspondence would be filed might be *Red* Feather Drive, *Fund* Raising, *Drive,* or *Community* Activities.

This example illustrates one of the main problems of subject filing — choosing the right classification.

A secretary or administrative assistant usually has the task of deciding on the classification name or descriptor for a subject file. Some are quite easy to select; for example, *Applications.* This subject comes to mind readily when one thinks about correspondence the boss may have had with people who are looking for work with his company. Many subjects, however, are not so easy to classify. Usually, therefore, a secretary might select subjects tentatively and let a little time pass to see how they work. If subjects chosen seem fuzzy and not easy to recall, she can revise them. For example, suppose she filed the boss's correspondence and documents about his car insurance under *automobile* but, as time passes, she finds that she nearly always looks first under the word *insurance;* in this case she should reclassify the folder. She may want to set up a subject "section" with *insurance* as a primary classification and subdivision folders (or cross references) behind it for *Business Cars,* (Personal *Automobiles*), *Fire, Health, Home, Life, Personal,* and *Theft.* Even telephone directories find it necessary to do quite a little cross referencing in their yellow pages. Notice this example taken from a telephone directory:

Academies —	Accordions
See *Schools*	Accountants — Public
Accident Insurance —	Acetylene Welding —
See *Insurance*	See *Welding*

As more and more subject classifications enter into your correspondence file, you may want to set up a separate subject file. This might be especially desirable if you are keeping files for a personal activity of the boss's not directly related to business. For example, suppose the boss has a farm where, as a hobby, he raises horses and cattle. Assume that he has collected quite a few clippings and pictures about prize-winning horses and cattle. Organizing these materials so that they would be useful and retrievable would surely require a separate subject file.

Even when a secretary is given the main responsibility for developing a subject classification and the boss rarely goes directly to the files himself, she should check the classification with him. After all, they are his files.

Requirements for a Good Subject Classification System

If the boss is the manager of a department in a large corporation and the subject file is integrated into that of the total corporation, the classification system may have been developed by a corporate-wide committee and may be standardized. But regardless of who makes the decisions about the subjects used, the first criterion of a good subject file is — Can you find the material when you want it?

Other guidelines for a good subject classification system are:

1. The subjects chosen should be short and to the point. Subjects of over three words should be avoided. Such a subject may indicate a need for a primary subject with subdivisions.
2. The subjects should be specific. Broad subjects such as *Meetings* or *Memorandums* do not work well. Use specific subjects as
     Meetings:
        Board
        Finance Committee
        Fund Raising
        Management Association
3. Subjects should be exclusive of others. They should not overlap.
4. Subjects should be clearly defined so that they are capable of only one interpretation.
5. The designer of the subject classification system should use the language of those who request the files.

Types of Subject Files

Except for numerical subject files, which will be discussed separately, subject files may be organized in one of two ways: (1) dictionary arrangement, or (2) encyclopedic arrangement.

1. Dictionary Arrangement for Subject Files

The dictionary arrangement is the straight alphabetical sequencing of subjects regardless of whether they are primary subjects or subdivisions. This is the way dictionaries list words; there is no attempt to group related subjects. Each subject is of equal importance with every other subject, and its relationship to certain other subjects is disregarded unless cross referencing is used. New subjects or subdivisions are added to the subject index in their alphabetic order. An example of a straight alphabetic subject file (dictionary arrangement) is shown in Fig. 6-1. This system is suitable for a very small subject file, probably no larger than one drawer.

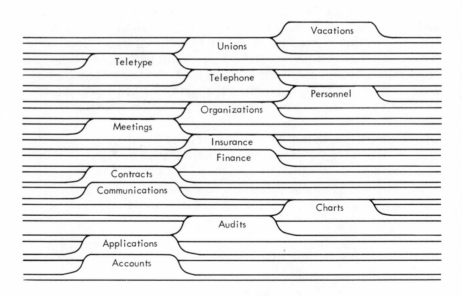

Figure 6-1. Dictionary arrangement of subject files

2. Encyclopedic Arrangement for Subject Files

With the encyclopedic arrangement, some subclassifications are grouped alphabetically under related primary headings. This is the way encyclopedias usually list their contents. If put into the encyclopedic system, the folders shown in Fig. 6-1 would be arranged as shown in Fig. 6-2. This type of subject classification works well if a file is no larger than three or four drawers. If it is larger, an alphanumeric or decimal system is recommended.

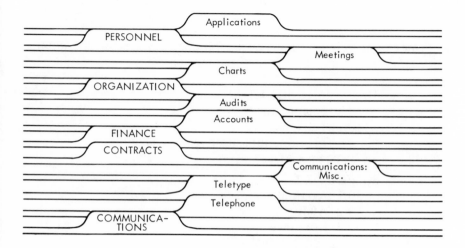

Figure 6-2. Encyclopedic arrangement of subject files

Numeric Subject Files

There are three types of *numeric* subject systems: (1) simple numeric, (2) decimal numeric, and (3) alpha-numeric. Numbers are added to subject indexing systems because some people find it easier to work with numbers. Numbers help to identify primary subject groupings and provide a network for expanding categories within the overall system.

1. Simple Numeric

Using the examples from Figs. 6-1 and 6-2 again, we could number the primary classifications as follows:

> 10 Communications
> 20 Contracts
> 30 Finance
> 40 Organization
> 50 Personnel

By numbering the primary subjects, we can now refer to them by either number or word.

2. Decimal Numeric

Our example, indexed in a decimal numeric system, would look like this:

        10 COMMUNICATIONS
            10.1 Telephone
            10.2 Teletype
                10.11 Communications (Miscellaneous)
        20 CONTRACTS
        30 FINANCE
            30.1 Accounts
            30.2 Audits
            30.3 Insurance
        40 ORGANIZATION
            40.1 Charts
            40.2 Meetings
        50 PERSONNEL
            50.1 Applications
            50.2 Unions
            50.3 Vacations

This system provides relativity in that the subtopics are related to the primary subject by having the same number to the left of the decimal point.

3. Alpha-Numeric

Alpha-numeric systems provide for escalated subdivisions of a topic and almost limitless expansion among related subjects. It is a useful system for a very large and growing subject classification; for example, the entire classification of medicine with all of its special branches and subdivisions, or the entire classification of medicines, drugs, and pharmaceutical supplies. To illustrate how the system might work, let us try to apply it to our example.

             10. COMMUNICATIONS
               10.1 Telephones
                 10.1a Commercial
                   10.1a1 Centrex
                   10.1a2 Intercom
                   10.1a3 PBX

10.1a4 Switchboard
10.1b Mobile
   10.1b1 Autos (Private)
   10.1b2 Planes
      10.1b2a Public
      10.1b2b Private
      10.1b2c Military
   10.1b3 Ships

A secretary is not likely to be involved in developing an alpha-numeric system such as this, but she may find it part of her job to work with one. In the small secretary-maintained files, it is not necessary to have both alphabetical and numeric designations. Alphanumeric indexes are usually prepared by specialists and a key to them is provided by a manual, handbook, or folder that contains a *relative index*.

Relative Index

If you can't remember the descriptor for a subject file, the relative index helps you find it. A relative index is a straight alphabetical listing of all the tab captions on the guides and folders in a subject filing system. It is like a city map; it shows you the whole thing. It is also used for cross referencing. Refer to the relative index not only when you want to find a subject descriptor but also when you have to add new folders so that the new topics will be correctly related to the rest of the system, without overlapping titles or duplicates.

Preparing Subject Files

If you find yourself involved in developing a subject file, here is a procedure to follow:

1. Assemble samples of the materials to be filed. Size up the project.
2. Develop a classification plan. Remember to make the descriptors short, meaningful, and in simple language.
3. Consult the boss.
4. Set the system up tentatively. You may want to use some old folders, anticipating that changes will be made.
5. Try the system for about four to six months.

6. Set up the system permanently but allow for future changes and additions.

7. Prepare a relative index for quick reference.

8. Code items for a subject file by encircling, underlining, checking, or writing in the descriptor. (See Fig. 6-3.)

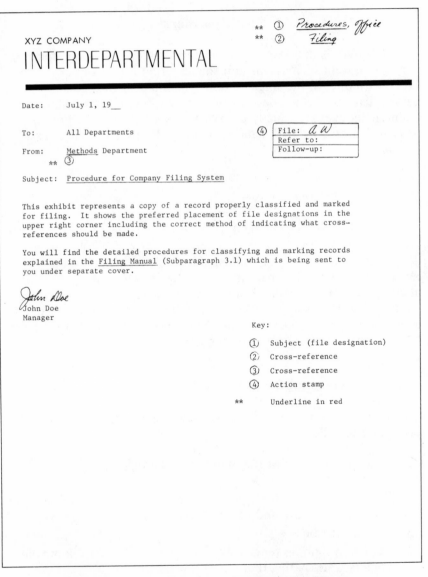

Figure 6-3. A memorandum coded for subject filing

Review Questions

1. What are the advantages of subject files?
2. What are some of the decisions a secretary must make in choosing classifications for a subject file?
3. What are some guidelines for a subject file?
4. When would you shift from a straight alphabetic subject file to the encyclopedic classification?
5. What is a classification?
6. What is the difference between a subject file and a relative index?
7. When only a few items are called for by subject, how do you provide for this in a regular correspondence file?
8. How would you go about developing a subject file for some personal materials in your boss's files?
9. Why use both numbers and alphabetic letters in a subject file?
10. How do you cross reference in a subject file?

Review Exercises

Review Exercise 1

a. You are employed in the personnel department. Code the items listed in the right-hand column using the relative index provided in the left-hand column. Some items may have more than one code number.
b. Prepare a suitable answer sheet.
c. Hand the answer sheet to the instructor for grading.

Relative Index: Personnel

1. Applications
2. Blood Donor Plan
3. Blue Cross and John Hancock Insurance
4. Contributions
5. Food Services
   5.1 Vending Machines

a. A new price list for Mars candy bars.

b. A written request from the office manager for tuition reimbursement for a night course in records management.

6. Hours of Work
   6.1 Holidays
   6.2 Vacations
7. Management Development
8. Medical Care
9. Performance Review
10. Recreation
11. Retirement
    11.1 Employee Length of
         Service
12. Safety
13. Salaries and Wages
    13.1 Incentive Plan
    13.2 Supplemental Com-
         pensation
    13.3 Workmen's Unem-
         ployment Compensa-
         tion

c. A clipping about
   another company's ex-
   perience with an em-
   ployee bowling club.
d. A memorandum to the
   manager of personnel
   about an article in
   Holiday magazine
   about group travel.
e. Notes and memos
   about setting up a Red
   Cross blood donor day.
f. A letter from the com-
   pany doctor about an
   employee who suffered
   a heart attack while at
   work. He recommends
   that the employee
   (who has been with the
   company for fifteen
   years) be given a part-
   time assignment for
   several months.

Review Exercise 2

a. Use the relative index on the left to code the twenty-five
   papers described on the right.
b. Prepare a suitable answer sheet.
c. After making the decisions necessary to code these
   twenty-five items, you have probably found some descriptors you would like to change. Name at least three
   you would like to change. Write the new descriptors on
   the bottom of the answer sheet.
d. Hand the assignment to the instructor for grading.

Relative Index   *Papers*

1. Administration   A. Program for annual
2.   Branch Office   National Records

3.   Projects Completed
4.   Projects in Process
5. Associations
6.   Conventions
7.   Meetings
8. Educational Institutions
9.   Colleges
10.   Universities
11. Equipment
12.   Chairs
13.   Posture
14.   Desks
15.   Modular
16.   Secretarial
17.   Filing Cabinets
18.   Card Size
19.   Correspondence Size
20.   Legal Size
21.   Machines
22.   Adding
23.   Bookkeeping
24.   Computer
25.   Typewriters
26. Government Contracts
27. Manufacturing
28.   Factory
29.   Employees
30.   Maintenance of
             Equipment
31.   Raw Materials
32.   Rent
33.   Production Schedules
34.   Production Statistics
35. Office Maintenance
36.   Heat
37.   Light
38.   Rent
39.   Supplies
40.   Stationery
41.   Envelopes
42.   Paper

Management Associa-
tion convention
B. Receipt for typewriter
repairs
C. List of local colleges
offering data process-
ing courses
D. Receipt for office rent
E. Ream of letterhead
paper
F. Plan for new factory
lighting
G. Union grievance report
on treatment of two
factory timekeepers
H. Brochure describing
posture chairs
I. Directions for operating computer
J. Measurements of space
occupied by legal files
K. Change in working
hours for factory em-
ployees
L. Contract for jungle
boots for soldiers
M. Schedule of freight
rates
N. Progress report from
subcontractor on Job
54
O. New supply of manila
envelopes
P. New procedure about
sending bulk mail to all
divisions of the cor-
poration
Q. Inventory of type-
writers

43.   Carbon
44.   Letterheads
45.   Second Sheets
46.   Ribbons
47. Transportation
48.   Express
49.   Freight
50. Water Rights for Factory

R. Analysis of costs of air conditioning computer room

S. Bill for pads to be placed under all typewriters

T. Report on number of shoes produced three years ago

U. Foreman's evaluation of workers' performance

V. Announcement of seminar of American Management Association on Reduction of Inventory

W. Bills of lading for goods shipped by freight

X. Standards to be followed in buying new typewriters

Y. Inventory of adding machines

Project 1. *A Subject File Coordinated with a Correspondence File*

Purpose: This project aims to:

1. give you further insight into working with subject classifications
2. help you develop judgment and experience in coding for a subject file
3. illustrate how a subject file can be integrated with a regular correspondence file
4. give you experience in coding correspondence for an alphabetic name file.

Materials: The following pages include twenty-eight letters and a relative index for a subject file. These are to be used in this project.

Setting: Assume that you work in the central files of D. C. Lloyd & Company, Denver, Colorado. Lloyd manufactures a variety of appliances such as amplifiers and micro-switches for electronic equipment. The company's main offices and factory are in Denver; a few dealers are scattered around the country, a representative "office" is located in Boston, and plans for a branch in Canada are under consideration.

The company follows a routine procedure of filing correspondence in two separate files: alphabetic by names of individuals and alphabetic by subject. An extra copy (photocopy duplicating process) is made of all correspondence, both incoming and outgoing, for the subject file. Although some in the Company regard this as a cumbersome system, the company's president has requested the subject classification back-up file for all correspondence because he thinks it facilitates a more thorough handling and better control of the many different types of items covered by the correspondence.

The twenty-eight letters you are to process for the back-up subject file consist of both incoming and outgoing correspondence.

Instructions:

1. Prepare a relative index as shown on page 126.
2. Read each letter and copy the number (see lower right-hand corner of each letter) on the relative index after the subject under which you think it should be filed.
3. Hand it to the instructor for checking.
4. Prepare a sketch of a file drawer with guides for twenty-one alphabetic divisions similar to the file-drawer sketches in Chapter 4. Combine I–J, Q–R, U–V, and XYZ.

   a. Reread the twenty-eight letters and code for the individual name filing system.

   b. On the guide tabs of your sketch, copy the numbers of the letters (see lower right-hand corner of each letter) to indicate the appropriate folder into which you think each piece of correspondence would be filed in an individual name filing system.

   c. Put your name on the sketch and hand it to the instructor for checking.

C   C
 A   O
  R   P
   B   Y
    O
     N

February 14, 19__

Mr. Keenan Doyle
359 South 40th #3
Aurora, Colorado

Dear Mr. Doyle

We have carefully reviewed your resume for participation in our
Accelerated Management Training Program. Your educational background
and interest in manufacturing have been important factors in our consideration.

In evaluating the total group of candidates, however, I find that we
are not going to be able to offer you a position at this time. With
your qualifications, I am sure you have a number of employment alter-
natives. I certainly wish you every success in the job you select.

Thank you for your interest in our Company.

Sincerely yours

Personnel Director

HGC:rh

1

UNITED STATES NATIONAL BANK OF COLORADO

MAIN BRANCH

6600 ARCADIA AVENUE
P.O. BOX 281
DENVER, COLORADO 80201

February 17, 19__

Mr. Vernon Pellatt
Finance Director
D. C. Lloyd and Company
934 West Van Buren Street
Denver, Colorado 80201

Dear Mr. Pellatt

This is in response to your recent inquiry concerning Signal Appliances, Inc., 2733 South Frontier Drive, Boulder, Colorado. Neighboring bankers contacted on your behalf tell us that the subject has been their customer since 1948, apparently maintaining throughout this time a deposit balance averaging in high four- and five-figure proportions. Credit, secured by accounts receivable, has extended to a high of a medium five-figure amount. A low five-figure amount is currently outstanding. Financial summaries of this company are not available to the bankers.

All banking relations with the company have reportedly been handled in a satisfactory way. Our information tells us that the company is an established one with a history of profitable operations. The bankers hold the subject responsible for normal business commitments.

We trust the foregoing information offered in the usual confidence will be of assistance.

Very truly yours

Wesley Addis

Wesley Addis
Assistant Cashier

wa/e

2

```
                                          C    C
                                           A    O
                                            R    P
                                             B    Y
                                              O
                                              N
February 23, 19__
```

Mr. L. B. Williams
Parker, Smith, and Aiken, Inc.
Investment Securities
1652 Blocker Building
Denver, Colorado 80201

Dear Mr. Williams

After our telephone conversation yesterday, I talked with our President, Mr. Channing Gregory, and he feels that the brokerage for the
sale and replacement of securities could be placed with your firm for
a stated period, say one or two years, but not in perpetuity.

Our securities are handled primarily through my department and change
from day to day. To pass all our security transactions through your
organization might be awkward and difficult. We find no objection,
however, to your suggestion that you inform us as to stock purchases
that in your judgment merit consideration.

I suggest that you prepare an agreement for the services you propose
and submit it to us for consideration. As I stated over the telephone,
I am not sure our set-up is such that we can advantageously use the
services of your company. However, we will be glad to review your
proposal and to cooperate with you, if possible.

Sincerely yours

Vernon Pellatt
Director, Finance and Investments

vp/rs

3

C
  A   C
    R   O
      B   P
        O   Y
          N

February 27, 19__

Mr. C. A. Price
Riley Manufacturing Company
Wilkes Barre, Pa.

Dear Mr. Price

This refers to your telephone call telling us that Order No. 14229, shipped the latter part of January, has not yet reached you. Apparently this shipment has gone astray. We are, naturally, sorry for the inconvenience this is causing you. We are putting out a tracer immediately.

In the meantime, we are air mailing a duplicate order that should reach you in a couple days.

Thank you for telephoning about the matter. We pride ourselves on giving good customer service, and it is only when customers keep us informed as you have that we can take remedial action. We assume that the air shipment will come through all right, but should you not receive it by the early part of next week, let us know.

Yours truly

H. T. Harris
Sales Department

HTH:ef

4

VANCOUVER TRUST COMPANY

571 Water Street
Vancouver 3, B.C.   268-1054
Canada

March 3, 19__

Mr. Channing E. Gregory
President, D. C. Lloyd & Company
934 West VanBuren Street
Denver, Colorado 80201

Dear Mr. Gregory

As I told you when we talked on the telephone this morning, Mr. Lee
Yetke (Canadian Pacific) and Mr. Stuart Chapman (Manufacturers
National Bank) have agreed to serve on the advisory board to consider
the advisability of locating a branch plant and/or a warehouse of
Lloyd's in this area. They are both well qualified.

I telephoned them after I talked with you to see about a meeting next
week and March 14 is a likely date. We can meet in my office at 9
that morning. I have also asked Larry Whitehead, a realtor, to meet
with us as he handles industrial sites. After lunch, we can go out
with him and look over several pieces of land he has in mind.

Will you bring a company lawyer or should I ask one of our lawyers
to sit in during the morning discussion? Unless you have some
special reason for not doing so, I advise using a Canadian lawyer for
obvious reasons.

We are glad to have been invited to work as your Canadian representative in this matter. We are also glad to know that Lloyd Company
is considering expanding into Canada. Where will you stay while in
Canada? Can our travel department help make reservations for you?
How many will be in your party?

Cordially yours

Horton Canfield

Horton Canfield
Executive Vice President

HC/dh

5

March 5, 19___

Reservations
Imperial Hotel
Vancouver B. C., Canada

Gentlemen

Please reserve 2 rooms, adjoining if possible, for the nights of
March 13 and 14. Mr. Channing E. Gregory, President of our company,
will occupy one, and two of our other men (Mr. Vernon Pellatt and
Mr. Kenneth Service) will share the other; twin beds please.

Their flight arrives in Vancouver at 3:07 p.m. March 13 so they
should be checking in around 4:00.

Please confirm the reservation.

Yours truly

(Miss) Maryanne Butterfield
Secretary to Channing E. Gregory, President

mb

6

```
        C     C
          A     O
            R     P
            B     Y
              O
              N
```

March 5, 19__

Mr. Horton Canfield
Executive Vice President
Vancouver Trust Company
571 Water Street
Vancouver 3, B. C., Canada

Dear Mr. Canfield

Mr. Gregory is out of the city today but asked me to write informing
you that he will be in Vancouver March 13, arriving on Canadian
Pacific Flight 607, 3:07 p.m. Accompanying him are Messrs. Kenneth
Service (Engineering) and Vernon Pellatt (Finance).

I have made reservations for them at the Imperial Hotel.

Yours truly

(Miss) Maryanne Butterfield
Secretary to Channing E. Gregory

mb

7

C
 A   C
  R   O
   B   P
    O   Y
     N

March 8, 19__

Mr. Ralph Wolfram, Contractor
Frontier Building
Juneau, Alaska

Dear Mr. Wolfram

Your letter and the 45-amp amplifier that you returned have been received. We have sent them to our engineering department so that the
amplifier can be tested. Your letter says it "blew" the works.
Previous laboratory tests of these amplifiers show they can stand
twice the load actually recommended for them. Only an excessive overload or a faulty part could have caused the damage you describe. We
will check exhaustively for both.

Since the tests may take up to four weeks, we will be unable to give
you a specific report until that time.

Yours very truly

Peter Hall, Manager
Services Department

PH/ad

8

ARMANDO de AMBRIEX
ENGINEER AND CONSULTANT
Praça deBriel, P 3a
Rio de Janeiro, Brasil   TELEFONE: 20-06-81

March 10, 19__

Accounting Department
D. C. Lloyd & Company
West VanBuren Street
Denver, Colorado

Dear Sirs

Recently I ordered some equipment from you and it arrived last week
safely. I have instructed my bank to send you a cashier's check in
the amount of $300 American dollars drawn to your honor.

I would appreciate it if, when you receive this check, you advise me
at once. Sometimes we have delays and complications in transmitting
monies to distant places. If this happens with the above cashier's
check, I would want to know as soon as possible so that I can start
tracing procedures and authorize a new document.

I am pleased with the equipment I received from your company.

Yours with regards

Armando de Ambriex
Sr Armando de Ambriex
Engineering Consultant

9

C   C
 A   O
  R P
   B Y
   O
    N

March 12, 19__

U. S. Department of Labor
Office of Labor Management
 and Welfare Pension Reports
Washington, D. C. 20210

Dear Sirs

Enclosed is a copy of our Employee Savings Plan Annual Report Form
for the contract year ending last December 31, file number WP 91-40-
57. This report covers our Employee Savings Plan for salaried employees with three years service.

Should there be questions relating to the report, please contact us.
If you need further information, let us know.

Yours truly

Personnel Department

HGC:rh

Enclosure

10

March 16, 19__

```
   C     C
  A       O
   R     P
    B   Y
     O
     N
```

Mr. Horton Canfield
Executive Vice President
Vancouver Trust Company
571 Water Street
Vancouver 3, B. C., Canada

Dear Horton

I have discussed with my executive committee various aspects of our
proposed plant in Vancouver. We discussed costs and financing, time
schedule, building restrictions, and economic growth factors. I
showed them pictures of the various building sites Mr. Whitehead
showed us, and they were unanimous in preferring the acreage off Highway 495 because of shipping connections.

The next logical step, it seems to us, is to have our production people
and architect develop a prospective building plan so that we can focus
in on real costs. With the continued rise in labor and building material costs, it may be that some additional financing will be needed
beyond the figures we discussed. I personally think we are being a
bit optimistic, and that our original estimate is too low. In any
event, we will plan to amortize the loan in the same period of time as
originally discussed.

What is the ceiling your bank will advance us? If we must go beyond
it, do you think Mr. Chapman's bank will be willing to get into the
picture?

Can you give us names and addresses of 3 building contractors so that
as soon as our architect has drawn plans and prepared the specifica-
·tions, we can submit them to the contractors for competitive bids?

I also discussed with my executive committee the matter of paying your
company a flat fee for its services in this matter rather than basing
it on the amount of the loan or on the total amount of our final investment. They agreed that this would be the most logical way to
handle it. We will pay in three installments: the first as soon as the
building plans are firm and all permits and legal documents are in
order; the second, at the completion of the structure; and the third
·3 months after the plant is opened. Let us know if this arrangement is
·not satisfactory.

Sincerely yours

Channing E. Gregory
President   11

CEG:mb

VANCOUVER TRUST COMPANY   268-1054

   571 Water Street
   Vancouver 3, B.C.
   Canada

March 19, 19___

Mr. Channing E. Gregory
President, D. C. Lloyd & Company
934 West VanBuren Street
Denver, Colorado   80201

Dear Channing

This replies to your letter of March 16.   I think your choice of acreage is a good one.

I have discussed with other people here at the bank the possibility of
your needing more money, and at present it doesn't look as if a larger
loan than the one we anticipate will be a problem--within limits, of
course. We should probably leave it at that, Channing, until your
architect draws up specifications so that we can get a stronger cost
picture.

Within a few days, we will send you the names of three contractors
we've worked with before. Insurance terms and a penalty clause
should be in the contract papers when bids are submitted.

The flat fee terms you describe are acceptable.

Cordially yours

Horton

Horton Canfield
Executive Vice President

12

ROBERTS, BESCH, CONDON, ADAIR, INC.

ATTORNEYS-AT-LAW

COMSTOCK BUILDING, N.E.
AIKEN, NORTH CAROLINA

March 22, 19__

Mr. Channing E. Gregory
President
D. C. Lloyd & Company
934 West VanBuren Street
Denver, Colorado 80201

Dear Channing

On behalf of the partners of Roberts, Besch, Condon, Adair, I want to
thank you for your thoughtful expression of sympathy on the death of
our senior partner, Mr. Daniel K. Roberts.

Our firm has suffered a great loss. He was one of the founders of
this organization and until just a few days before his death, continued to be a strong and respected voice in it. We hope to carry
on in the fine example and tradition which he established for us.

Sincerely yours

Dennis

T. Dennis Besch
Partner

tdb:lc

D. C. LLOYD & COMPANY MEMO

To: All Department Heads   Subject: Dennison copiers

From: Geo. Vaughn, Administrative   Date: March 25, 19__
       Services

May I have your cooperation, please, on an important office service
item? Costs incurred in using the Dennison copiers that are available throughout the Company are extremely high and increasing every
month. The time has come to examine how this equipment is being used
by each department and to control its abuse.

Several departments are going to channel all copy work through a secretary. One is going to log-in all the work done on the copiers.

We feel that some type of control is desirable in order to cut down
on unnecessary copying.

14

April 8, 19__

Mr. Oha Wakun
Director, Department of Commerce
State of Hawaii
Division of Securities
Honolulu, Hawaii

Dear Oha

Thank you for your nice telephone call in answer to my appeal for new
ideas about handling credit procedures. It was certainly a pleasure
to talk with you; I enjoyed our conversation.

You may recall that I was interested in the fact that banks in Hawaii
are apparently unwilling (or prohibited by law; you weren't sure)
from giving out credit information. As I indicated to you, I have
been wondering what approach to take here at Lloyd's to open up ave-
nues to obtain the information we need more quickly. I am not yet
satisfied that the best way to solve our dilemma is through Dun and
Bradstreet.

You may remember that we talked of a possible "Code of Ethics" among
manufacturers for the exchange of credit information. Adherence to
such a code, if it could be established, would enable manufacturers
with similar types of customers to exchange information with confidence. I believe the National Retail Credit Association, which is
comprised of retail credit grantors throughout the country, has a
code of ethics for the exchange of credit information. Such a system
should work particularly well if computerized.

As any person engaged in credit work well knows, unless you can get
accurate and adequate information about a potential customer fast, it
is impossible to make a sound credit decision. I'm sure everyone
knows the tremendous importance of accurate credit information and
the impact it has on the well-being of a company. If we could establish a good credit system among manufacturers such as they have in
other "industries," we would be able to help each other all over the
world. For example, suppose a business in Italy placed an order for
$3,000 or more with us. As the situation now stands, we have to con-
tact someone in Italy (usually a bank) and hope they'll take time to
give us the information we need and that when and if it comes, it
will be accurate. Obtaining credit information about foreign customers is particularly difficult because they don't seem to realize
that we do hold such information in the strictest confidence.

Oha, I sincerely appreciate your ideas and help in this matter. It
was a pleasure to talk with you. I send best wishes to you and yours.

Sincerely yours

                                                                           15

Vernon Pellatt
Director, Finance and Investments

April 8, 19__

Simpson and McGregor Publishing Company
Wayne Building, Suite 17
Tuscaloosa, Alabama

Gentlemen

Please send us an examination copy of your new book by M. Iris
Greene, In-House Development Programs. ·Bill the company, not
Mr. Cutler. Thank you.

                    Yours truly

                    Helen Gettis (Mrs.)
                    Secretary to Harry G. Cutler
                    Director of Personnel

hg

                                                            16

C   C
A   O
R   P
B   Y
O
N

April 8, 19__

Mr. Shannon Grillo
Vice President and Manager
Credit Department
First National Bank of Denver
Denver, Colorado

Dear Mr. Grillo

I want to thank you for the pleasant and helpful visit I had with you
in your office yesterday. I appreciated the opportunity to talk with
you because you have such a wealth of experience and knowledge in the
credit field.

After talking with you, I am convinced the best approach to solving
our problem is to revise the credit procedure we are now using. For
one thing, it takes us too long to establish a new customer's credit
and no doubt we lose business as a result. You discussed some of
these things so convincingly that I've decided to present some of the
points you made at the next meeting of our executive committee.

I wonder if, at your convenience, you would give me a letter supporting the need to speed-up the credit-check procedure and explain
how some of your ideas work and save time. I would appreciate your
permission to use the letter with our executive committee, if necessary.

Sincerely yours

Vernon Pellatt
Director, Finance and Investments

VP:i

17

C   C
A   O
R   P
B   Y
O
N

April 10, 19__

Mr. Ralph Wolfram, Contractor
Frontier Building
Juneau, Alaska

Dear Mr. Wolfram

The 45-amp amplifier that you returned last month has been carefully
and extensively checked in our laboratory. We found nothing defective.

As stated in our March letter, this equipment will stand twice the
load we actually recommend for it so the situation in which it de-
faulted for you must have been a case of excessive overload.

We are returning the amplifier to you today believing that it is in
perfect condition and that it should serve you well, if properly used.

Yours very truly

Peter Hall, Manager
Services Department

PH/ad

18

SIMPSON AND McGREAGOR PUBLISHERS, INC.

17 WAYNE BUILDING

TUSCALOOSA, ALABAMA

AREA CODE 205
262-8471

April 11, 19__

Mrs. Helen Gettis
Secretary to Mr. Harry G. Cutler
Director of Personnel
D. C. Lloyd & Company
934 West VanBuren Street
Denver, Colorado 80201

Dear Mrs. Gettis

We have sent you a complimentary copy of M. Iris Greene's new book,
IN-HOUSE DEVELOPMENT PROGRAMS. As soon as Mr. Cutler has examined
it, write us what he thinks about the book, whether he plans to use
it, and how he will use it.

We will not reprint any part of your evaluation without first clear-
ing it with you. We are asking for Mr. Cutler's opinion because we
have just newly launched into this area of publication--training--
and want to get as much feed-back from customers as possible.

Thank you for helping us.

Cordially yours

I. K. Benson

I. K. Benson
Industrial Text Division

IKB:p

19

A & D RAILWAY

ADOLF & DOUGLAS ARNOLD, PROPRIETORS

MAIN TERMINAL: 46 COTTAGE STREET, SHARON, MASSACHUSETTS 02067

STATION MASTER PHONE: 617-784-6993

April 16, 197_

D. C. Lloyd & Company
934 West VanBuren St.
Denver, Colorado

Gentlemen

Copies of the No. 6229A special freight shipment schedules that you
asked for in your letter of April 8 will be sent to you within the
next day or so.

We hope they are clear and that we may have the pleasure of being of
further service to you.

Very truly yours

Don Morrison

Don Morrison
Supervisor, Freight Shipping Division

DM/jtb

20

ALUMNI OFFSET, INC., LITHOGRAPHERS

175 Varick Street, New York, N.Y. 10014
Telephone: 924-1150

April 17, 19 _

Mr. Peter Hall, Manager
Services Division
D.C. Lloyd and Company
West VanBuren
Denver, Colorado 80201

Dear Mr. Hall

I will be in Denver May 12 and 13 and can be available to discuss
with you the publication of the brochures about which you wrote our
Chicago office last week.

Could you suggest a convenient time? I do not know yet what interview schedule our Denver office has arranged for me, but will work
in whatever time you suggest. Perhaps you should, if possible, suggest an alternate time.

I am looking forward to meeting you.

Sincerely yours

H. J. Donahue

Harry J. Donahue
Sales Representative

hjd:r

21

C C
A O
R P
B
O
N Y

April 18, 19__

Mr. Ron Johnson
Production Manager
Skagway and Sons, Inc.
Minneapolis, Minn.

Dear Mr. Johnson

Since receiving your letter of April 9, we have scoured our records
and warehouse looking for a reference to the material you say arrived
defective and which you returned. Our suggestion is that you send a
tracer out after this shipment. In the meantime, we do not feel we
can issue a refund until we see the returned merchandise.

We regret this delay and can only hope that you see our point of view.

Yours very truly

Jordon W. Gardner
Sales

JWG:h

22

STANDISH ENGINEERING ASSOCIATES, INC.

Suite 17, Marshall Building
Austin, Texas 78703

AREA CODE 512

581-0663

April 19, 19__

Mr. Don Slatter
Data Processing
D. C. Lloyd & Company
934 West VanBuren Street
Denver, Colorado 80201

Dear Don

I'm writing to congratulate you upon being awarded the Distinguished
Service Award for outstanding contributions in the Computer Association of America.   It is a tribute to you, an honor to your company,
and recognition of your many activities in CAA.

Congratulations on an outstanding career in data processing.

Yours sincerely

Dan

Dan Sears
2nd Vice President
Computer Assn. of America

23

D. C. LLOYD & COMPANY MEMO

To: All Department Heads   Subject: Administrative Manual

From: George Vaughn, Ad. Services   Date: April 21, 197_

Recently the firm of Place and Fujita, Records Management Consultants, proposed that they provide a consulting service in assisting the D. C. Lloyd Company in establishing a records management program. A presentation covering a variety of functional disciplines, including files management, retention scheduling, inactive records storage, forms management, and the development of an administrative manual, will be made to our management staff.

Arrangements have been made to discuss this proposal with Place and Fujita in Conference Room 2 at 10:00 a.m. on Wednesday, April 28.

President Smith has requested that all department heads attend this meeting.

24

A F C CORPORATION

REFRACTORIES FOR INDUSTRY

April 22, 19_

Mr. Ken Service
Manager, Engineering Division
D. C. Lloyd Co.
934 West Vanburen Street
Denver, Colorado 80201

Dear Sir

I noticed in one of your bulletins that you have started some new
product developments that you expect to complete in a year. You
may know that the AFC Corporation has, for years, helped companies
such as yours facilitate new product programs.

I have asked our Colorado representative to call on you to explain
our services. We hope you will find time to talk with him.

Yours very truly

J. Dan Edwards

J. Dan Edwards
Executive Vice President

hz

25

WESLEY ARCHER & SONS

242-2345

AREA CODE 304   MANUFACTURERS OF INDUSTRIAL SUPPLIES

PENOBSCOB INDUSTRIAL PLACE

HUNTINGTON, WEST VIRGINIA

May 19, 19__

Mr. Arthur Bailey, Jr.
Plant Production
D. C. Lloyd and Company
VanBuren Street
Denver, Colorado

Dear Sir

I met a representative of yours at a Manufacturers Association regional
meeting, and I described to him some equipment that we need in one of
our new plants. By the way, your man was Harry Fisinger. I believe
he is with your Engineering Division.

I have checked the catalog and price list he gave me and the amplifier
parts are listed as Aa3a, Parts 6a, 14d, and 1-01b. I would like six
of each. We will appreciate prompt shipment.

Yours truly

Larry Erickston

Larry Erickston
Plant Production

le-aj

26

DENTON CORPORATION MONTEREY & CASTLE ROADS   MEMPHIS, TENNESSEE 38102

May 28, 19__

Research Department
D. C. Lloyd & Company
934 West VanBuren Street
Denver, Colorado 80201

Gentlemen

I work in the engineering design division at Denton Corporation, and
while at a regional engineering meeting in Mobile last week, heard
of some unique research your company is doing on switching circuitry.

Can you send me a copy of your findings please.

Yours truly

E. Hughes

Eugena Hughes (Mrs)
Research Associate

27

SCATLAN INDUSTRIES

BANGOR, MAINE

AREA CODE 207
263-5963

June 12, 19__

Mr. Peter Hall
Services Division, Lloyd & Co.
934 VanBuren Street
Denver, Colorado

Dear Sir

I am writing with reference to some equipment we purchased from your
firm about a year ago. Your advertisements guaranteed complete sat-
isfaction. I'm sorry to report, however, that our experience with
the equipment has not been satisfactory.

We installed the deluxe model AA3 amplifier and related control panel
with the extra sets of micro-switches tied in from remote stations.
The sound effects have been noisy from the very beginning and the
low-to-medium dial settings do not adjust properly. Your service representative out of Boston was up twice to check the unit. In spite
of his servicing, the installation does not operate satisfactorily.

Since we installed the unit in the home of an important and much
respected citizen, and he has an expensive and extensive recording
system connected to it, we are embarrassed about the trouble he has
had with it. I think the public-relations effect of this situation
is important enough for you either to send us a complete replacement
of your equipment (which will be tricky, at this point, to install)
and/or send us one of your servicemen who knows more about the equipment than the man from Boston appears to know.

Yours truly

Ken Towers

Ken Towers
Building Contractor

28

Relative Index for Chapter 6

1. *Branch Plants*
   a. Canada
   b. United States
2. *Data Processing*
3. *Development*
   a. Exhibits
   b. Facilities
   c. Produce (See Research)
   d. Research (See Product)
   e. Program
4. *Federal Reports*
5. *Finance*
   a. Accounts Receivable
   b. Accounts Payable
   c. Budgets
   d. Credit (general)
   e. Insurance
   f. Investments
6. *Miscellaneous*
7. *Office*
8. *Orders*
   a. Back Orders (See Delays)
   b. Delays (See Back Orders)
   c. Credit Information
9. *Personnel*
   a. Applications
   b. Appreciation (See Congratulations)
   c. Condolences
   d. Congratulations (See Appreciation)
   e. Education
   f. Health
   g. Policies
10. *Red Feather Drive*
11. *Security*
12. *Service*
    a. Complaints
    b. Customer
    c. Order Adjustments
    d. Production
    e. Shipments

7

Numeric Filing Systems

In numeric filing systems items are classified by number instead of name. There are several reasons why numeric systems are preferred over other systems.

1. When names in an alphabetic correspondence system are assigned numbers, there are two ways to file and to look for them (name and number) so that papers are less likely to get lost. This is important in certain types of records, such as medical files.

2. Many classification systems are computer-oriented. Computers process numbers more efficiently than alphabetic characters. Computer systems analysts say that each piece of information can be represented by a number and every number can be represented by a hole on a punched card or a magnetic spot on tape.

3. Some business records are traditionally handled by numbering systems: order forms, parts and inventory items, catalog items, purchase requisitions, to name a few. Such items are numbered because they generally do not relate primarily to persons.

4. Records in professions, research, and some businesses group themselves around cases. For example, medical or dental records or insurance cases. Number systems help to batch such records.

5. There is a certain amount of secrecy in numeric systems because the identity of the person to whom a numbered folder applies is known only to those who know the system. An example is Swiss banks where accounts are identified only by number, thus assuring secrecy.

Sometimes numeric systems are integrated into individual name correspondence systems. For example, in a very active file, when a folder reaches its capacity and a new one is made, the two folders are then numbered in sequence and dated. Or, a very active file might be subdivided with monthly folders, 1 through 12. Follow-up files also use 1 through 31 (days of the month) numbering systems. Subject files may also use numeric systems in this way.

Basically there are two types of numbering systems: (1) serial or sequential: 1, 2, 3, 4. . . and (2) coded or significant.

Serial Numeric Filing Systems

The simplest numeric system involves numbering items consecutively. For example, when a new patient is admitted to a medical center, he is given the next available number. His record is then filed by number and cross referenced to his name. When another automobile comes off the production line, it is assigned the next available number. All shipping records, correspondence with dealers and similar transactions use this number. When records are numbered consecutively (11943, 11944, 11945 . . .), it seems that they should also be filed in serial sequence and that is exactly what is usually done.

Coded Numeric Filing Systems

Some companies do not like straight sequential numbering systems, which they regard as nonsignificant numbers or convict systems. Such numbers, they say, do not tell anything about the item being filed. For example, a straight sequential product number doesn't tell anything about the size, capacity, model, or function. But coded numbers do.

Both letters and numbers can be used in a code. Codes are sometimes called mnemonics. *Mnemonic* is an adjective meaning that which helps someone remember something. For example, states use mnemonics in license number systems. The first digit may indicate cities in order of their size, and the second indicates the county. Hence, a Nebraska car license, No. 1–1–830, would be decoded as Omaha (largest city in Nebraska, therefore No. 1), and Douglas County (one of the counties in the area covered by Omaha, hence also assigned No. 1). There are, of course, many other ways of coding license numbers. Social security and zip code numbers are other examples of mnemonic numbers, sometimes also referred to as "significant" numbers.

Block Codes

A block code is a simple refinement of a straight sequential numbering system. Blocks of numbers are set aside for items that have a common characteristic. For example, Nos. 1–25 might be set aside for all accounting forms in a company, Nos. 26–50 for all advertising department forms, 51–75 for administrative forms, and so on. Such numbers soon become identified with the departments to which they are issued so that, at a glance, when you see Form 3–ag–14, you know it is from the accounting department.

Numeric-Name Filing Systems

When name folders in a file are also assigned numbers, the primary guides carry numbers. (See Fig. 7–1.)

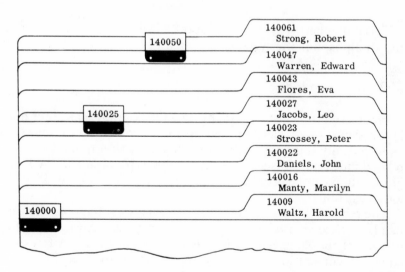

Figure 7-1. A numeric-name file

Miscellaneous folders may be used in a numeric-name system just as they are in alphabetical correspondence filing systems. One miscel-

laneous folder may be put in for each primary guide; when there are
five or so papers for a newly issued number, an individual folder
should be made. Folder labels should show both the name and the
number. Such a system is feasible in a medical center where records
might be a matter of life or death. This double filing classification
cuts down the chance of filing errors. Folders are numbered to correspond to the guides and are placed behind them in numeric sequence.
Guide and folder tabs may be straight line or staggered arrangements.
One guide is recommended for every five to ten folders. Primary
guides are numbered in the hundreds or thousands, and the secondary guides, in tens or hundreds. For example:

	Primary Guides	*Secondary Guides*
Hundreds	100	110,120,130,140,150,160,170,180,190
	200	210,220, etc.
	300	310,320, etc.
Thousands	4000	4100,4200,4300,4400,4500,4600,4700,4800,4900
	5000	5100,5200,5300, etc.
	6000	6100,6200,6300, etc.

Serial numbering systems can also be expanded through the decimal or alpha-numeric systems discussed in Chapter 6.

Related Card Index

Since even the most remarkable memory cannot remember numbers assigned to a variety of records, some type of related index filed
alphabetically is usually necessary when numerical filing is used. A
related index on cards is the most flexible type, although the index
information can be listed in a book (an accession book) or kept in a
loose-leaf folder.

The related index is used in the following way. Suppose the cases
in a law office are filed by a serial number system. A file folder for
new client Harold J. Harney is assigned number 81522. A few days
later, a document for the Harney case arrives at the files. Because the
folders are filed numerically, not alphabetically, if the correspondent
did not thoughtfully write the case number on the document, we
must look it up in the related card file. There we should find a card

like the one shown in Fig. 7–2. A relative index card must always be made when the number is assigned. It should show the name and address of the client and the number assigned to the folder. Other useful information may be added.

Name: *Harvey, Harold J.*	File Number:
Address: *406 Evans Ave. Columbus, Ohio*	*81 522*
Acct. Opened: *1/7*	Related File Nos: *10520* *72461*
Subject: *Pension Plan Laws*	*no court action*
See: *Ohio Statute 43-LP-06* *Mich. " 94-PLS-618*	

Figure 7-2. Related index card

Terminal-Digit Filing

A problem with serial numeric filing is that, over the years, numbers assigned may run into six and seven digits. Furthermore, many records are retired to storage, thus creating gaps in the numbering system. The more items there are in a serial file, the harder it is to file them accurately. To make matters worse, the most recent additions will have the longest numbers and probably will be the most active.

Terminal-digit filing was developed to overcome the problems of serial numeric filing in large systems. The terminal-digit filing system is simple. The numbers are filed backward. That is, instead of filing 377343 as is, the number is read from right to left and broken into primary and secondary groupings: 43 (primary guide), 73 (secondary guide). (See Fig. 7–3).

If a terminal-digit system has 100 primary guides (00, 01, 02, etc.), the system has a total of 10,000 guides (100 x 100). A smaller system with 10 secondary guides (0–9, 10–19, 20–29, 30–39, etc.) behind each primary guide, would contain 1,000 guides.

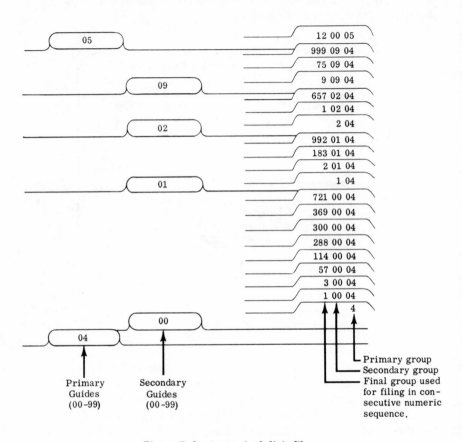

Figure 7–3. A terminal-digit file

Because terminal-digit systems are usually large, shelf files are often used for them. A secretary is not likely to develop or keep a terminal-digit system in her office. Yet, since many large companies, especially insurance and manufacturing companies, use terminal-digit systems, she at least should understand the rationale of the system. Figure 7–4 illustrates equipment that might be used for a large terminal-digit system, which combines hanging folders, the open-shelf idea, and motorized equipment.

Figure 7–4. A motorized terminal-digit filing system
(*courtesy White Machine Co.*)

Date Files

Date files (also called chronological files) are used for follow-up, suspense, or tickler systems. Tickler systems "tickle" the memory on the date an item needs attention. Calendar tickler systems and small card-size tickler systems for out-files are usually maintained by a secretary.

A tickler file can be set up for almost any filing system. For example, when used for out-files, it reminds the secretary when the item should be called back to the files. When used with a direct-name alphabetic correspondence file, it calls attention to follow-up action that should be taken on a letter. An extra copy of correspondence is all you need for a correspondence-size tickler system that is kept separate from the main filing system. Physically, a tickler file can be merely a series of thirty-one guides or folders numbered consecutively and kept separate from the main file. It can be either a set of folders or a card file.

Card-file Tickler

In a card tickler system memos can be dropped loosely behind the numbered guide cards. The entire system can be kept in a file box in the secretary's desk.

Folder Tickler

For a folder tickler system, special celluloid-edged folders with movable signals may be used. (See Fig. 7–5.)

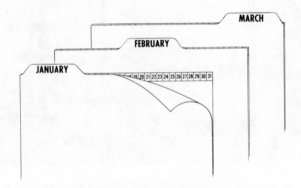

Figure 7–5. A date-tickler file
(*courtesy Shaw-Walker Co.*)

Sets of date guides can, of course, be inserted behind special or individual guides and folders in correspondence filing systems. Such a set can be a series of twelve (for the months) or 4 weekly: 1–8, 9–16, 17–23, 24–31, depending on the number of items to be filed.

Tickler systems, no matter what the type, are important supplemental filing systems.

Review Questions

1. What is a numeric filing system? Give an example.
2. What are the advantages of numeric filing systems? What are the disadvantages?
3. What is a serial numeric filing system?

4. Describe a situation where a serial numeric system might be used.
5. What is a coded numeric system?
6. Describe a situation where a coded numeric filing system might be used.
7. What are the advantages of a serial numeric filing system? What are the disadvantages?
8. What are the advantages of a coded numeric filing system? What are the disadvantages?
9. Why are numeric systems sometimes used with alphabetical name systems?
10. Why does a numeric filing system need a "related" file? Give an example.
11. What is terminal-digit filing? Give an example of how it works.
12. What is an advantage of terminal-digit filing? What is a disadvantage?
13. What is a tickler system?
14. Describe a type of tickler file a secretary might keep.
15. Give three examples of mnemonic code systems you encounter in your daily life.
16. How are miscellaneous items handled in numeric filing systems?
17. If a social security and a zip code number are mnemonic, what do the various digit positions mean? How do these mnemonic systems work?

Review Exercises

Review Exercise 1

a. Find dictionary definitions for the following terms.
b. Type the definitions neatly, use each term in a sentence about office work, and hand the exercise to your instructor for checking.

1. Mnemonic codes
2. Nonsignificant numbers
3. Relative index
4. Serial numbering
5. Consecutive numbering
6. Sequence
7. Ordered numbering
8. Significant numbers
9. Terminal-digit numbering
10. Tickler files

Review Exercise 2

    a. Arrange the following numbers for terminal-digit filing.
    b. Type the list of numbers twice: once for consecutive se-
       quence filing and once for terminal-digit sequence filing.
    c. Hand the exercise to the instructor for checking.

1.	531,603	5.	83,678
2.	54,484	6.	313,639
3.	224,083	7.	152,809
4.	843,278	8.	353,834

Projects

Project 1. *Follow-up*

Purpose: This project aims to:

    1. help you develop judgment in estimating follow-up
       time;
    2. give you experience with a follow-up file.

Instructions: Assume the items listed below are on your desk to be
           marked for the tickler file.

    1. Indicate the appropriate follow-up date for each by
       checking in the appropriate column.
    2. Prepare an appropriate answer sheet and submit it to the
       instructor for checking.

	3–7 days	*2–3 weeks*	*Other (Explain)*
a. Notes for an article for a yearbook.			
b. A letter from a prospective graduate assistant.			
c. A committee report. The next meeting is the week after next.			

	3-7 days	2-3 weeks	Other (Explain)
d. Notes for a special lecture to be given in four weeks.			
e. An announcement about a student-faculty seminar to be held in ten days.			
f. A letter from a professional group asking for a conference as soon as possible.			
g. A note about arranging a meeting in three weeks for a visiting professor from Ghana.			
h. A note about a conference with the dean after some departmental enrollment data can be prepared.			
i. A report from a professional association with material in it to be reproduced for use in a large seminar scheduled for the last week of the semester — ten weeks hence.			
j. A schedule of information about a workshop being planned by your department. The workshop will be held in four weeks.			
k. Information for the faculty yearbook.			

	3-7 days	2-3 weeks	Other (Explain)
Publication deadline is in one month.			
l. A reminder to update library material for next year's courses.			
m. A note about revising course descriptions.			
n. A note reminding the professor about a speaking engagement in six weeks.			

Project 2. *Terminal Digits*

Purpose: This project aims to:

1. help you understand better the concept of terminal-digit filing.
2. give you experience in working with a numeric filing system.
3. give you experience in working out a multiphased project.
4. help you, once again, to review the rules for alphabetizing names.

Instructions: Project 2, Chapter 2, contained forty names that were to have been alphabetized. This project should have been returned to you by the instructor. Correct any items that were wrong so that the list is in alphabetic order.

1. Assign the following customer subscription numbers to the original forty alphabetized names on the list you prepared in Chapter 2.
2. Convert the newly numbered items to a terminal-digit system.
3. Draw a terminal-digit system like the one shown in Fig. 7-3. Make it large enough to handle forty items.

4. Print ("file") your list according to the terminal-digit system.

5. Type the list of names in the order they appear when filed by the terminal-digit system.

6. Hand the project to the instructor for checking.

1. 59565	11. 50490	21. 41340	31. 86436
2. 74617	12. 24899	22. 85252	32. 80402
3. 92043	13. 60192	23. 82759	33. 63183
4. 50279	14. 24910	24. 98383	34. 20035
5. 80184	15. 57466	25. 79051	35. 39500
6. 57755	16. 44700	26. 73978	36. 93613
7. 64595	17. 72615	27. 21090	37. 27342
8. 77534	18. 88396	28. 94088	38. 81281
9. 73988	19. 86480	29. 78666	39. 49428
10. 30381	20. 99682	30. 48283	40. 41729

8

Geographic Filing Systems

In addition to the ways we have already discussed, records can be classified by geographic location. Geographic filing is an alphabetic arrangement by location – state then city. The primary guides are states, although if international correspondence is involved, they might be countries. The divisions of a geographic file depend on the type of business and the way the files are used. If it is a local business, the primary guides might even be counties or boroughs; the secondary might then be cities and villages. The advantage of geographic filing is that it groups related materials by location.

Geographic filing is useful in many different situations. Sales records, weather records, market research, and ecology studies are but a few examples of the types of materials that need to be filed by location. It should be observed here that not all geographical files are necessarily written records. A geographic file might be different colored tacks stuck into a wall map in the boss's office. For example, suppose your boss is a state highway engineer and one of his "files" is a large mounted highway map that hangs in his office. The map shows where bridges are located on the highways of your state and the types of bridges they are. Blue-headed tacks designate bridges under 100 feet long; black ones, two-way bridges; and yellow ones, four-lane expressway bridges. Such a map-and-tack record becomes a geographic *information system* with classifications highlighted through color coding. Information can be "retrieved" from it at a glance if you know the classification system used.

Geographic File Arrangements

Information should be classified the way it will be called for. Because correspondence probably will be involved in any geographic files that a secretary is likely to keep, provision should be made for both individual name folders and geographic guides.

Geographic guides may be integrated into correspondence files in two ways: (1) with the *state* primary and *city* secondary guides arranged on the left side of the drawer and the individual name folders on the right; (2) with state, city, or county guides inserted behind special name guides or behind individual name folders for expansion. (See Fig. 8-1.)

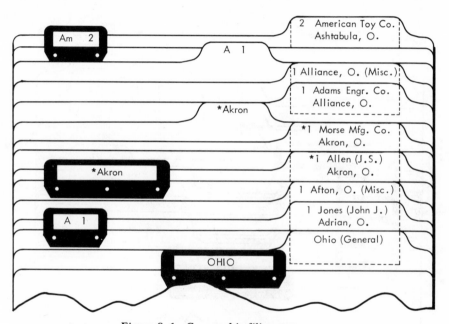

Figure 8-1. Geographic filing systems

Figure 8-1 provides only a few illustrations. There are many possible arrangements of guides and folders in a straight geographic file or in a combination geographic and individual name file. An important guideline in creating such a system is, "Keep it simple." Do not introduce unnecessary color coding, numbering systems, or special guide subdivisions.

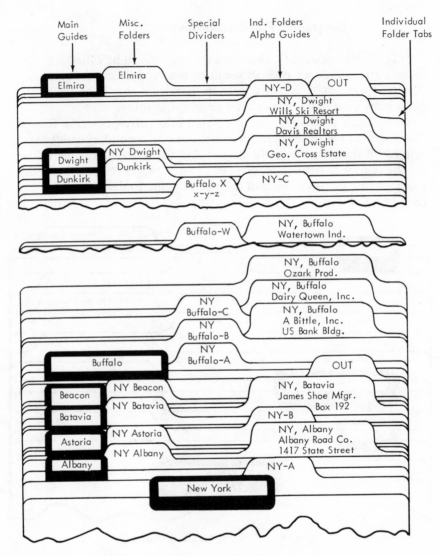

Figure 8-1 cont.

Cross Reference

When both geographic and individual names are used in a filing system, they automatically provide, to some extent, their own cross references. Some regular cross referencing is still necessary though. Remember that a copy of the item itself is usually more effective as a

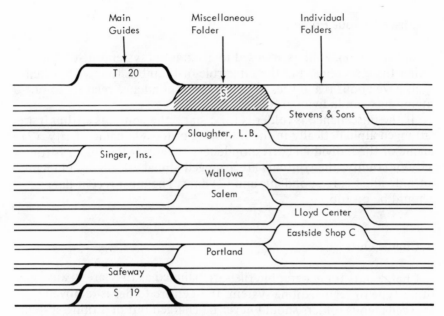

Figure 8-1 cont.

cross reference than a cross-reference sheet. Extra copies are easy to make with today's easy-to-use copying equipment.

Whether you make a copy or fill out a cross-reference sheet is a matter of judgment. If most of the cross referencing is between individual name folders and geographic folders, it may be helpful to set up a card index by names of individuals or businesses (Safeway, Inc., for example) and do the cross referencing on the cards. List on the card the locations of Safeway stores with which you are corresponding. (See Fig. 8-2.)

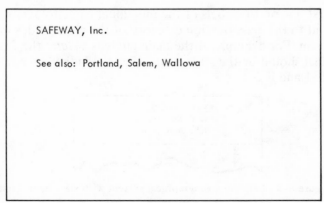

Figure 8-2. Cross-reference card

Miscellaneous Folders

Miscellaneous folders are used in geographic systems just as in
other filing systems, and the same rule-of-thumb is followed: When
you have about five pieces of active correspondence relating to one
item, make an individual folder.

If the miscellaneous folder is for a state, the contents within it are
arranged alphabetically in the following order: (1) name of city, (2)
name of the individual correspondent, (3) date. If the folder is for a
city or county, the contents are arranged alphabetically by (1) name
of individual correspondent, and (2) date. The most recent date
should be on top.

Charge Outs

Charge outs for geographic files are handled as they are in any
other type of regular filing system. If an entire folder is removed
(miscellaneous folders should *never* be charged out of a filing system),
and the account is very active, a substitute charge-out *folder* may be
used in which to store new items as they come in while the original
folder is out. Otherwise, insert a charge-out card with an OUT-tab
that protrudes conspicuously. Out guides are usually lined up in one
position within the system. If only one document is removed from a
folder, a charge-out *sheet* may be used. Here again, a conspicuously
protruding tab is recommended, and color coding should be used.

Labels

The first line on the labels of the individual name folders should
correspond to the classification category of the main guides in the
filing system. For example, if the main guide is a *state,* the first unit
on the label should be the state name. (See the individual name labels
in Figs. 8–1 and 8–3.)

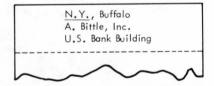

N.Y., Buffalo
A. Bittle, Inc.
U.S. Bank Building

Figure 8–3. Label in a geographical system with state name first

It always speeds up file handling to underline the first filing unit on the label.

Sorting

If a filing system is geographically oriented (main guides are *states*), rough sort by state and fine sort to the individual folder names. If the filing system is individual name-oriented and only a few geographic guides have been inserted for emphasis or expansion, sort alphabetically by names of individuals first.

Review Questions

1. When is geographic filing useful? Describe two situations in which businesses are likely to use geographic files.
2. When might a secretary insert some geographic guides into a regular alphabetic correspondence name filing system?
3. What problems do you see in mixing geographic guides into a regular alphabetic correspondence name filing system?
4. When do you issue "individual" folders in geographic filing?
5. How are charge outs handled in geographic filing?
6. What is geographic filing?
7. What is a map-and-tack geographic file?
8. Describe a business situation in which a map-and-tack geographic file should be used.
9. What do you see as a disadvantage of a map-and-tack file? What is an advantage?
10. How do you handle miscellaneous items in a geographic filing system?
11. How are letters arranged in miscellaneous folders in a geographic filing system?
12. How do you cross reference in a geographic filing system?
13. When might you use a supplementary card system in geographic filing?
14. What is the best way to arrange information on an individual name folder in a geographic file?
15. How would you sort items for a geographic filing system?

Review Exercises

Review Exercise 1

  a. Prepare a suitable answer sheet for this exercise.
  b. Answer each of the following fourteen items with a
     yes or *no.*
  c. Hand the assignment to the instructor for checking.

Example: In a geographic file you would file: *Answer*

  x. Mamie W. Lasonde, Aspen, North Caro-   x. __no__
     lina, after Lasons Service, Aspon, South
     Carolina
  1. Eisenberg Furs, Pratt City, Oklahoma, be-
     fore Eisenberg, R. L., Piper Lake, Ohio?
  2. The Four Ed's Restaurant, Brooklyn,
     New York, before The Four-Forty Grill,
     Brooklyn, Michigan?
  3. Lane-Bender Associates of Scranton,
     Pennsylvania, before Lane Bryant of
     Scranton, Pennsylvania?
  4. Neo-Art Studio, Wheeling, West Virginia,
     before Neo Classical Art Studios, Inc.,
     Wheeling, West Virginia?
  5. Kel-Mer Van Corp., West Port, New York,
     after Kelmer's Bargain City of West
     Point, New York?
  6. Fiberbilt Sample Case Co., Arlington,
     Missouri, before Fiber Case Novelty Co.,
     Arlington, Massachusetts?
  7. National Bank of Detroit (Michigan) be-
     fore National Bank of Butte (Montana)?
  8. The Iberia Air Lines of Spain, New York
     City, before Iber-American Distributing
     Company of New York City?
  9. Lady Lyda Corp. of Johnson, Vermont,
     before Lady Lyda Capers Cookies, John-
     son, Virginia?

10. LaCloche D'Or Cafe, Leeds, Massachu-
    setts, before Mrs. D. LaCloche, Lees,
    Massachusetts?

11. Jacob Rice Glass Company, Eden, Ken-
    tucky, before J. C. Rice, Edan, Kentucky?

12. Paulette Rheem of East Town, New York,
    after Paula Rhem of Easton, New York?

13. N.Y. Philharmonic-Symphony Society,
    New York, before N.Y. Phoenix School
    of Design, New York?

14. Progressive Electronic Contractors Cor-
    poration, Uptown, New York, before
    Progressive Electronics Company, Up-
    town, North Carolina?

Review Exercise 2

a. After each group, indicate the order in which the
   names given should be arranged in a geographic
   file.

   Example: (a) Helen's Dresses, Coleville,
   Ohio; (b) T. P. Helverson, Coleville, W.
   Va.; (c) Helen Heller, Coleville, Okla-   *Answer*
   homa.   a, c, b.

b. Prepare a suitable answer sheet and give it to the instructor for checking.

1. (a) New London Grill, Albany, N.Y.; (b)
   Newton Park, Albany, Oregon; (c) Vicki
   Upton, Albany, New York.

2. (a) Jerry Jake Koepka, Dorrance, Florida;
   (b) J. J. Kinder Supplies, Dorrence, Florida;
   (c) Keinder & Sons, Inc., Dorrance, Kansas.

3. (a) Brown Florists, Beaverton, Maine; (b)
   J. G. Brown, Beaverton, Oregon; (c) John
   Brown, Bellmont, Oregon.

4. (a) Twenty Club, Manhattan, N.Y.; (b)
   Twenty-one Club, Manhattan, New York;
   (c) Twin-Pack Biscuit Company, Manhattan, Kansas.

5. (a) The Land of Donuts, Bloomfield, Ill.;
   (b) Carl Lamb, Bloomfield, Illinois; (c)
   Lamb's Motel, Bloomfield, Ill.
6. (a) Henrietta S. Clair, St. Clair Shores,
   Michigan; (b) St. Clarica's School, St. Clair
   Shores, Mich.; (c) H. T. Claire, St. Claire,
   Montana.
7. (a) Carlton-Winston, Attys., Toledo, Ohio;
   (b) Calahan Winston, Toledo, Ohio; (c) Carlton Realtors, Toledo, Oregon.
8. (a) Chi Company, Winston, N.C.; (b) Lee
   Chin, Winston-Salem, North Carolina; (c)
   The Chin Foundation, Winston, N.C.
9. (a) Bell and Jean's Cafe, Wichita, Kansas;
   (b) The Bill & Jean Nurseries, Lawrence,
   Kansas; (c) The B J G Company, Lawrence-
   berg, Kansas.
10. (a) Sears-Roebuck, Ville Platte, La.; (b)
    Mary Robeck, Platte, Nebraska; (c) Katie
    Sears, Plattsburg, Vermont.

Projects

Project 1. *Updating Subscriptions*

Purpose: In this project, you handle the subscription files for a
              professional journal that your employer edits. It is en-
              titled *Quick Thoughts* and you have accumulated ten
              additions and corrections to be added to the file. This
              project aims to:

1. give you experience making changes in a subscription
   file;
2. review the filing and indexing rules for name files;
3. alphabetize geographically;
4. plot data geographically on a map of the United States;
5. compile a little data from the "file";
6. give you experience working with a card file.

Materials: On page 150 you will find a map of the United States
              divided into five areas: Northwest, Southwest, Central,

Northeast, and Southeast. Following the instructions for this project, you will also find forty names and addresses of subscribers to *Quick Thoughts.*

Instructions:

1. Prepare forty index cards with the names and addresses.
2. Alphabetize the forty cards:
   a. Rough sort by state.
   b. Fine sort where there are two or more cards for a guide.
   c. Make a set of guides by pasting "tabs" to regular cards. Insert the individual name-and-address cards behind the guides.
3. Update the file by writing the following corrections on the appropriate cards:

   Changes
   a. Change Belle Meachim's subscription (Fairfield, Conn.) to 88 Phillips, Bridgeport, Conn.
   b. Change the spelling of Abrons House, Miller, Nebraska, to Abrown House.

   Additions
   1. George Fink Industries, Satlow Drive, Fort Atkinson, Wisconsin
   2. General Offices, Adam's Brush Company, 14 Mullett Drive, Lynwood, California
   3. Horological Works, Inc., 15 Castle Building, Richmond, Virginia
   4. Kriwow Farms, Inc., Denver, Colo.
   5. Highway Transportation Study Headquarters, N.Y. Metropolitan Region, 201 Park Avenue, New York, New York
   6. Roland Walton, 731 Amsterdam Avenue, Miami, Florida
   7. Robert Rogoff, 691 State Building, Duluth, Minnesota
   8. Theo. Quarg, 105 Mill Road, Scranton, Pennsylvania
4. Prepare index cards for the above additions. File them.
5. Print in the names of the states on the map. (Write your name and the date on the map.) Then, with a colored pencil, plot the distribution of the subscriptions you have for twenty-three states by placing a dot or *x* at the

appropriate location. (This part of the exercise simulates working with a map-and-tack file.)

6. Prepare a brief summary statement showing the total number of subscriptions by state and area: Northeast, Central, Northwest, Southwest, and Southeast. Give the summary an appropriate title; date it and write your name on it.

7. Hand the completed project (cards and summary) to the instructor for checking.

Figure 8–4. Map of the United States

Subscribers to *QUICK THOUGHTS*

1. Mrs. Mario Buccellati, 705 Plaza Street, Black Hills, South Dakota.

2. Dennis Horowitz, 277 First Avenue, New York, New York

3. Vincent Finn and Son, One Madison Street, Cleveland 15, Ohio

4. Mrs. Lolita Roche Diaze, 17 Sherwood Road, Ypsilanti, Michigan

5. The Culver Fabrics Shop, 4518 So. 69th Street, San Antonio, Texas

6. Henry Csigay, 1543 Marlboro Blvd., Superior, Wisconsin

7. The Eastside Methodist Church, 70–74 Carling Blvd., Minneapolis, Minnesota

8. Barney Cuccioli, 60 Riverside Drive, Freeport, Maine
9. Camp Na-Wa-Kwa, Sheridan Lane, Bangor, Maine
10. Hayes Malcolm, Manhattan Drive, Fort Lauderdale, Florida
11. Michael Malge, Corning Road, Orange, Texas
12. The Maline Associates, Inc., 4633 Tower Building, San Francisco, California
13. The Ponce DeLeon Hotel, Fairfield, Florida
14. Smilow-Thielle Furniture, 1860 Cresset, Chicago, Illinois
15. The United Ignition Corporation, 11352 Chambers Building, Detroit, Michigan
16. The United Nations Mission (Pakistan), 8 East 65th Street, NE, Washington, D.C.
17. United States Academy Motel, Highland Falls Road, Arlington, Virginia
18. Office of the Auditor General, United States Air Force, 641 Washington Street, New York City
19. United States Coast Guard Base, St. George Bay, Long Island, New York
20. Administrative Office, National Aeronautics and Space Administration, Western Division, Olympia, Washington
21. Harkness Naval Base, Floyd Bennett Field, Brooklyn, New York
22. Wright Paterson Air Base, Columbus, Ohio
23. The National Bank of Pueblo, Pueblo, Colorado
24. US Projector Corporation, WOW Building, Des Moines, Iowa
25. J. C. McWade, Hanson Blvd., Albuquerque, New Mexico
26. Miss Belle Meachim, Gold River Drive, Fairfield, Connecticut
27. Mathew McO'Neal, Greview Road, Long Beach, California
28. The In Friendship Cafe, Commerce Building, Philadelphia, Pennsylvania
29. The In-Tag Suppliers, 18285 Archer Building, Dallas, Texas
30. J. G. McOrlly, 4200 East Washington, Butte, Montana
31. McSorels Old Timers Inn, Galesburg, Illinois
32. Al Horswell, 4829 South Blvd., Beverly Hills, California

33. Karl Fink, M.D., 140 Medical Center, Boston, Massachu-
    setts
34. Mary Bubniak, Professor of History, University of Ne-
    braska, Lincoln, Nebraska
35. Mrs. Shirley Buchalter, West End Avenue, Beacon Hill,
    Massachusetts
36. Jack Adams, M.D., 14 Hilton Road, Bradford, Pennsyl-
    vania
37. The Abrons House, Miller, Nebraska
38. The Academy of American Poets, 1078 Madison Avenue,
    Shelby, North Carolina
39. Cooper-Bessemer Corporation, General Offices, Scran-
    ton, Pennsylvania
40. Geneno Brothers, Realtors, Acme Building, Jacksonville,
    Florida

Zip code numbers have been omitted to make Part 6 of the project more meaningful.

Project 2. *A Name File*

Purpose: In this project, you work in the office of the director of
a gallery of contemporary art who accumulates correspondence and reference materials in an extensively subdivided, direct-name file as illustrated. The first
thirty-two drawer fronts of the total system are shown.
Below are the names of forty artists whose correspondence is to be filed. This project aims to:

1. help you review the direct-name filing rules;
2. work with an extensively subdivided filing system.

Instructions:

1. After each of the forty items in the given list, indicate
   the number of the file drawer it goes into.

                                                         Answer
   Example: D. L. Derizinski   13

2. Using the file drawer numbers as guides, type the names
   in alphabetic order. Type the first filing unit, first, in all
   capital letters or underlined. Give the exercise a title.
3. Hand the typewritten list to the instructor for checking.

Aa–Al 1	Bar–Bd 5	Caa–Cd 9	Daa–Dn 13	Fi–Fq 17	Haa–Hem 21	Jo–Jz 25	Ku–Kz 29
Am–Aq 2	Bea–Bk 6	Ce–Cn 10	Doa–Dz 14	Fr–Fz 18	Hen–Hol 22	Ka–Kd 26	Laa–Ln 30
Ar–Az 3	Bl–Bq 7	Coa–Coo 11	Ea–Eq 15	Ga–Gq 19	Hom–Hz 23	Kea–Kol 27	Loa–Lz 31
Bas–Baq 4	Bra–Bz 8	Cop–Cz 12	Er–Fh 16	Gra–Gz 20	I–Jn 24	Kom–Kt 28	Maa–Mn 32

1. Kirkby, Donna   _____
2. Garlough, Glenn   _____
3. Duer, Albrecht   _____
4. Beuerle, Reuben   _____
5. Cotterman, Mayme   _____
6. Friedrich, Caspar   _____
7. Antones, Rachel   _____
8. Mao, Philip   _____
9. Borch, Gerard   _____
10. Haythorn, George   _____
11. Grimmer, James   _____
12. Blaschak, Arlene   _____
13. Djeduski, Stanley   _____
14. Gauntlett, Edgar   _____
15. Hecht, Bonny   _____
16. Cebulkey, Sue   _____
17. Anttonen, Gwen   _____
18. Dworkin, Cal   _____
19. Cloke, Della   _____
20. Lochner, Stefan   _____
21. Felbeck, Tena   _____
22. Isenbrant, Adriaen   _____
23. Cheever, Reva   _____
24. Atkins, Hugh   _____
25. Hoagbin, Naomi   _____
26. di Pietro, Sano   _____
27. Ivany, Dorothy   _____
28. Kishimoto, Ya   _____
29. Fukano, Mao   _____
30. Memling, Hana   _____

31. Gaede, James   _____
32. Jeserich, Paul   _____
33. Martini, Simone   _____
34. Kirchner, Ennid   _____
35. Courtney, Ashley   _____
36. Feallock, Bette   _____
37. Matsys, Quinten   _____
38. Leestma, Leo   _____
39. McArdle, Lyod   _____
40. Enid, Helen   _____

9

Card Filing Systems

The previous chapters in this Workbook have discussed correspondence and document files. Card files have been mentioned only as supplementary systems for other systems of filing. In this chapter the focus is on *card* files as such. There are many types of card files, all meeting different needs. Special systems and special equipment have been developed to house them and simplify their handling. Card files have been motorized and automated.

Card files generally have the following advantages:

1. A card is a separate, durable unit on which information can be accumulated.
2. Cards of the same size are easy to handle in batches.
3. Card systems are easy to keep in sequence. It is easy to add them or take them out of a file.
4. Card systems are easy to manipulate. It is easy to add to or take information from them.
5. Cards make good *unit* records.
6. Some types of cards can be used with machined or automated data processing systems.

Card systems are used in all businesses. They are used to accumulate information about customers, transactions, sales territories, and products. Cards may be filed geographically, numerically, by date, or by subject, although most manual card systems are alphabetic by individual name. Cards for automated systems are usually numbered. Regular filing, indexing rules, and practices are used, although punched cards for electronic data processing systems may be in random order; that is, they do not need to be sequenced according to the indexing rules and practices presented in this workbook. Cards in manual systems also may be cross referenced. Tab signal systems may be set up in card filing systems similar to those used in folder files. (See Fig. 9-1.)

Figure 9-1. Flexindex
(*courtesy Oxford Pendaflex Corp.*)

A guide should be used in manual systems for about every twenty to twenty-five cards. Card-size guides are available with the same type of alphabetic breakdowns used in folder files in sets ranging from twenty-three guides to thousands. (See Appendix, Standard Divisions for Alphabetic Guides.) Standard sets for 60, 100, 150, and 200 dividers are available.

Cards

Cards can, of course, be cut to any size, but there are several standard sizes: 5" by 3", 6" by 4" and 8" by 5". Traditionally, we write across the breadth of a card, but there is no reason why we cannot turn cards and write across them lengthwise.

Cards can be ruled or plain; they can be colored or white. They can be specially designed for various types of information.

Designing Cards

When designing a card for a filing system, consider the amount of information that will go on it, the type of filing equipment in which it will be used (typewriters, for example), the method of posting variable information to it, whether it will be ruled or plain, how it will be used, and whether it will be handled and removed from the file often. Many card files contain preprinted forms. The preprinted items are called *constant* data and the items that are to be posted to the cards are called *variable* data. (See Fig. 9-2.) Cards should be designed so that the variable data are easy to post and retrieve.

AMERICAN RECORDS MANAGEMENT ASSOCIATION 15th NATIONAL CONFERENCE
Century Plaza Hotel, Los Angeles, California

Name: (Mr./Mrs./Miss) _____

Company Name: _____

Address: _____

City: _____

State/Prov. _____ Zip _____

ARMA Chapter: _____ Non-Member ☐

My wife is registering: Yes ____ No ____

If yes, her name is _____

SEMINAR AND TOUR REGISTRATION
Monday, Oct. 12 (See Program)
    AM (Write In) _____
    PM _____
Tuesday, Oct. 13 (See Program)
    AM (Write In) _____
    PM _____
Wednesday, Oct. 14 (See Program)
    AM (Write In) _____
    PM _____

REGISTRATION FEES

FULL CONFERENCE Members ☐ $ 90.00
Fee includes reception, seminars, Non-Members ☐ $125.00
luncheons, and banquet.
NOTE: $35.00 of non-member registration
may be applied toward ARMA membership. ☐
Check here for application.

ONE DAY REGISTRATION ☐ $ 40.00
Fee includes seminars and luncheon on any day of attendance.
BANQUET ☐ $ 15.00
LADIES PROGRAM ☐ $ 30.00
Fee includes: Tour through Universal Studios and Beverly Hills,
A Harbor Tour, A special seminar on "Record Keeping in the
Home," evening social events, and banquet.

SPECIAL EVENTS AND TOURS
Arrangements will be made for special events scheduled through Thursday,
October 15. Please note your preference. The cost is not included in
registration fee.
Disneyland ☐   Knott's Berry Farm ☐   Marineland ☐

PAYMENT OF FEES
Make check or money order payable to: 1970 ARMA National Conference and
mail to: Worldway Postal Center
                P.O. Box 90550
                Los Angeles, California 90009
For additional registration forms, write amount here. _____

Your Pre-Registration Becomes Part of the Earlybird Drawing

Figure 9-2. Convention registration: a preprinted card

Another consideration in designing cards is how information will be recorded on them — longhand, typewriter, or punched holes. If drawers of files need to be carried from one desk to another in an office, cards may be punched at the bottom and fastened into a drawer with a rod the same way guides are sometimes fastened into file drawers.

Types of Card Systems

Vertical Card Files

In vertical files, cards stand on edge. Vertical card files are very compact, but when information is posted to them manually, the card must be lifted out of the file and placed on a flat surface for writing. This takes time and extra work space. For this reason, *visible* filing systems should be used when information is to be added to the cards often. *Vertical* card file systems are best for reference work, such as the card catalog in a library where space is a factor.

The main caption on a card should be in the upper left corner, since this is the easiest spot to see when you thumb through a file of vertical cards. (See Fig. 9–3.)

WORLD Affairs Council

Room 72, 461 N.E. Yamhill Road
Poughkeepsie, New York

J. M. Baker in charge of programs.
Vickie Strozio, assistant to Baker.

Figure 9–3. A reference card

Wheel Card Files

A ready reference card file often found standing near a telephone is a little wheel file. (See Fig. 9–4.) The cards are easy to reference by just spinning the wheel, and new data usually can be added without removing the card from the wheel.

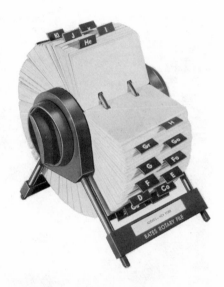

Figure 9-4. A handy reference rotary desk file
(*courtesy The Bates Manufacturing Co.*)

Wheel files come in many different sizes suitable for cards that
hold entries of 4 or 5 lines up to large sizes that hold 8" x 5" cards.
Large cards are suitable for accumulating case records such as medical
histories, research projects, or investments. Small wheel files for a
few hundred cards may be kept on top of a desk or near the telephone, whereas desk-height wheels that handle thousands of large
cards may be made a part of a secretarial work station and kept within easy reach.

Visible Card Files

Cards in visible files are stored flat in tray-like drawers and fanned
out with overlapping edges. (See Fig. 9-5.) The "overlap" leaves
a *visible* margin, which is how this card system gets its name.

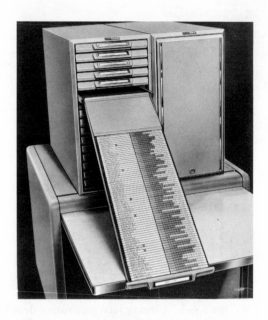

Figure 9-5. Part of a visible card file with signals to indicate
such things as due date, credit limit, special terms, and the like
(*courtesy Acme Visible Records, Inc.*)

    Visible cards can be stored in various types of equipment – trays,
narrow flat drawers, books, or panels. Regardless of how they are
stored, they all have the same advantage of quick access. The most
important items are written on the visible margin at the bottom of
the card so that the indexing information is visible at all times. (See
Fig. 9-5.) Another advantage of visible files is that those stored in
flat tray files are ready for posting by just lifting the cards ahead of
the one on which you want to record additional information and
posting the new entry. (The cards fit on a trunnion wire, as can be
seen in Fig. 9-6.) This feature of visible filing is a great time-saver.

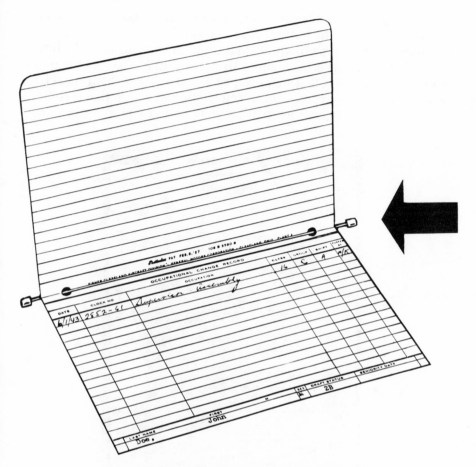

Figure 9-6. Postindex system showing trunnion wire
and entry on visible (lower) margin
(*courtesy Datavue Products Corp.*)

Signals. Another special advantage of visible files is that they are
easy to signal. Tabs can be attached to the visible strip in any position
or color. In a subscription file, for instance, a red tab might mean
that the subscription is due, and a yellow tab might signal that this
subscription is for a school to which copies are mailed in bulk. A tray
full of such signals can be read at a glance and special items can be
spotted quickly.

When typing a visible card, put the indexing captions and signal code areas as near the bottom edge as possible.

Mobility. One type of visible files often used for name and address listings or price lists is made up of strips. In addition to total visibility, another advantage is that items can be added easily without breaking alphabetic or numeric sequence. Merely pull out a strip that is to be removed or push two strips apart to make room to insert a new one.

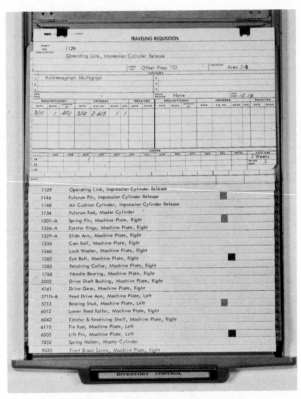

Figure 9-7. Close-up of a visible index panel ready for photographing

Applications. The card-filing concept is used for addressograph cards, punched cards, related indexes, and cumulative records where items are regularly posted to master cards. A secretary will use card files to the extent that she is responsible for working with such records. She may find several types of card files in her office, or she may take the initiative and develop some for charge outs, frequently used telephone numbers of correspondents and callers, personnel records, or a reference bibliography for the boss. If new items are to be added to the cards from time to time (for instance, research or project records), she may want to consider using a visible system with signals. Whatever the need or type of equipment used, she should keep the system simple. Avoid the temptation to dress up a filing system of any kind just to make it look impressive. A dressed up system usually takes more time and work to maintain.

Review Questions

1. What are the advantages of card files?
2. What are the advantages of vertical card files? The disadvantages?
3. What are the advantages of visible filing? The disadvantages?
4. What are the advantages of wheel files? The disadvantages?
5. For what types of filing systems is a secretary most likely to use cards?
6. What guidelines should be used in designing card filing systems?
7. What is constant data on preprinted card forms? Variable data?
8. What are some standard card sizes?
9. How do signaling systems differ for vertical and visible cards?
10. Describe two types of visible card files.

Review Exercise

a. This exercise is divided into two sections. Prepare a suitable answer sheet for it.
b. For the ten true-false statements, indicate answers either with a *T* or *F*. For the second part, type answers, using short, direct sentences.
c. Hand the answer sheet to the instructor.

I. True or False

1. Records are all documents recorded on paper.
2. Filing is the classifying and arranging of collected information for reference and preservation.
3. The word "file" comes from the Latin word meaning *system.*

4. Many filing systems use color to make them attractive.
5. Tabbed folders in staggered positions take up additional space.
6. Hanging folders collect dust.
7. When papers are taken or borrowed from a folder, they should be marked in red.
8. Vertical file cards are filed on edge.
9. It is easy to post additional data to wheel card files.
10. An advantage of visible files is that they are easy to signal.

II. Complete

1. In your own words, define *filing*.
2. In your own words, define *records*.
3. List three advantages of card files.
4. List three advantages of visible files.
5. List two advantages of wheel files.

Project 1. *A Card File for Catalogs*

Purpose: In this project, you are a records clerk in the purchasing department of an airplane manufacturing company. You have been working with various catalogs of different sizes and thicknesses. You decide that a related card system of some type would make it easier for you to work with the catalogs; there are about eight hundred of them. About fifteen hundred different items are ordered from the thousands of articles described in the catalogs. This project aims to:

1. give you a systems design problem to think about and solve on your own;
2. give you experience in designing a card file form;
3. give you experience in setting up a card system.

Materials: You need a few 5" by 3" cards for this project, a ruler for measuring space, and a sheet of paper on which to draw a sketch of the filing system.

Instructions:

1. Design a system to file and control the use of eight hundred catalogs of various sizes, ranging from ¼ to ½ inches

in thickness. Describe (or sketch) the equipment for the catalogs themselves, pointing out any special features such as color coding.

2. Design a card system for quick reference to information the catalogs contain. Either sketch the card on a sheet of paper or type (or print) the actual form on a 5" by 3" card.

3. Hand the finished project to the instructor for checking. Be sure your name is on it.

10

Maintaining and Controlling Filing Systems

It is said that nothing stands still; it either moves ahead or backward. Like everything else, filing systems, once they have been set up, need to be maintained. They need to be updated from time to time as the nature of the contents changes and new equipment is developed. New guides may be needed; miscellaneous folders may be needed; individual folders and labels may need to be replaced.

Periodically, older records must be separated from active ones. Some should be thrown away, but most should be transferred to make way for the new. Obviously, there is only so much space in an office that can be given over to files.

> *General Rule*
>
> Move unused materials out of active, working files as fast as possible. Establish a routine procedure for doing this.

Moving old files to storage also makes the active ones easier to find. It helps to maintain efficiency. It has been said that on the average only 67 percent of the files need to be retained in the office itself. Others can be moved to storage.

Transfer Methods

Records can be classified as *active* and *inactive.* When records become inactive, they should be moved. One reason for transferring old files is to put them into less costly storage. (See Fig. 10-1.)

> *General Rule*
>
> Separate closed or inactive files from active ones.

Collapsible transfer files are made of cheaper materials than active files. They are usually corrugated fiberboard boxes that can be assembled as needed. (See Fig. 10-2.) Storage boxes are available in letter size, legal size, tabulator card size (either with lift-off lid or tie-down flaps), and check sizes. Factors to consider when buying storage boxes are:

1. Are they one-piece construction?
2. Do they have carrying handles?
3. Is the lid dustproof?
4. Is there wax on the bottom so it will slide easily on shelves or in storage frames?
5. Are corners reinforced or protected?
6. Is there a place for a front identification label?
7. How high can they be stacked without sagging if not stacked on shelving?
8. If contents require limited access, what security features do the boxes have?
9. How fireproof are they?

Surprisingly, corrugated fiberboard boxes, especially double thickness ones, protect records quite well from the effects of sprinkler systems and controlled fires. Paper chars at 350 degrees and corrugated fiberboard does not transmit heat as much as metal does. Uninsulated metal cases transmit heat quickly so that paper contents of metal cases become charred as they would in an oven.

Figure 10-1. An example of storage equipment for punched cards
(*courtesy Oxford Pendaflex Corp.*)

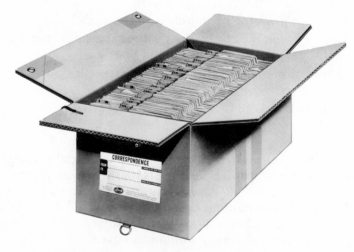

Figure 10-2. Corrugated storage box
(*courtesy Bankers Box Co.*)

> *General Rule*
>
> File vital and security-classified materials accordingly. For instance, use fire resistant file cabinets.

There are two general transfer methods: — *perpetual* and *periodic.*

Perpetual. Perpetual transfer means that papers are being transferred out of active files all the time, either as they become inactive or whenever the secretary or filing personnel has time to do it. Perpetual transfer is mostly used for case histories, medical records, legal records, and research and construction projects where papers are not easily separated from the main file while the projects are active. Instead, the records are transferred in total as projects are finished.

Periodic. Periodic transfer means that papers are transferred at stated intervals and at definite times. Many offices like to transfer at the end of the fiscal year. Some secretaries like to transfer while the boss is on vacation. There are three periodic transfer plans: (1) one-period, (2) two-period, and (3) maximum-minimum period.

1. When the *one-period plan* is used, all the contents of a file except the guides are transferred. The advantage of this plan is that decisions about what should be transferred do not have to be made. Everything goes! The disadvantages are that toward the later part of the period inactive files will have accumulated in the active files and that active files will be transferred along with inactive when the transfer is made.

2. More realistic is the *two-period plan.* This is the same idea as the one-period plan except that the records are transferred to an easily reached location. For example, since the middle two drawers of a four-drawer cabinet are easiest to reach, contents from drawer 2 are moved to drawer 1; contents of drawer 3 are moved to drawer 4; and contents from drawers 1 and 4 are stored nearby. At the next transfer period, contents of drawers 1 and 4, are moved to less accessible storage, drawers 2 and 3 move into drawers 1 and 4, and a fresh start is made in drawers 2 and 3.

3. Under the max-min plan, maximum and minimum transfer periods are set, based on a study of the file contents. When the max period expires, papers dated prior to the min period (say 6 months) are transferred. This leaves in the files only those papers bearing the min period dates. For example, let us set the max at 1 year and the min at 6 months. We transfer materials out of the files every 6 months. On transfer day, January 2, 1973, we transfer everything dated before July 1, 1972. On July 1, 1973, we transfer everything dated before January 1, 1973.

Retention Schedules

Looking through files and trying to decide what should be transferred is a tedious task. It is better to follow a definite retention
schedule of some sort. If, for example, you know that accounts
payable records are to be transferred 3 months after date paid, you
are more likely to transfer them at that time than if you leave it to
chance. A retention schedule sets up target dates.

> *General Rule*
>
> Every office needs a simple set of
> guidelines (preferably in writing) to use
> in deciding which items to file, which
> items to move to storage, which items
> to microfilm, and which to throw away

Sample retention schedules are available from filing supply and
equipment houses. Merely ask your local office supply company for
one. However, each office should develop its own retention schedule
based on a study of how much the records are used and upon legal
factors, especially the statute of limitations. A sample of a short,
generalized retention schedule is given below.[1] See the Appendix for
a more detailed one. Some retention schedules are 50 and more pages
long.

A. File in wastebasket: Routine inter-office memoranda as soon as
   acted on; incoming mail of no importance, such as announce-
   ments; form letters; all superseded papers, pencil notations, etc.

B. File one month: General correspondence requiring no follow-up.

C. File three months:
   1. Incoming and outgoing correspondence with customers on
      routine, promptly settled business.
   2. Incoming and outgoing correspondence with vendors on
      routine, promptly settled business.
   3. Stenographers' notebooks.
   4. Receiving tickets.
   5. Purchase requisitions.
   6. Packing slips.
   7. Bank statements.
   8. Expired insurance policies.

D. File two years:
   1. Work sheets for financial statements.

---

[1] Adapted from materials supplied by Records Control, Inc.

    2. Internal reports and summaries, including output from data-processing equipment.

    3. Physical inventory tags and summaries.

    4. Punched cards and tapes for various purposes.

E. File to comply with the statute of limitations in the states affected.[2]

    1. Cancelled payroll checks and summaries.

    2. Invoices to customers and from vendors.

    3. Data on ex-employees.

    4. Duplicate deposit tickets.

    5. Completed contracts and leases.

    6. Accident reports.

    7. General releases in lawsuits.

    8. Time cards and tickets.

    9. Cost compilations and audit reports.

  10. Assignments and attachments.

F. File permanently:

    1. Books of accounts; minute books.

    2. Capital stock ledgers and transfer records.

    3. Cancelled checks, vouchers, and cost data on capital improvements.

    4. Deeds, mortgages, and other conveyances or lien instruments on real property.

    5. All tax returns and related papers.

    6. Maps, profiles, specifications, plans.

    7. Perpetual agreements regarding pensions, group insurance, and other fringe benefits.

    8. All property records.

Disposition

Records need to be disposed of. Businesses cannot keep all the records they use. However, someone with authority and experience should decide what records to destroy and when to destroy them. A secretary should set aside records she thinks might be destroyed and check them with the boss at an appropriate time. In some instances, authority should be in writing. It may be desirable, in fact, to keep a

[2] The statute of limitations specifies the time limit within which an action may be brought upon a contract. It varies among the states. For instance, if a creditor does not assert his claim on a written contract in Missouri within ten years, it is said to be outlawed and his right to bring action will be barred. In Oklahoma, on the other hand, the statute of limitations begins to operate after five years. The statutes of limitations have a great effect on the retention schedules of companies doing interstate business. The best legal minds are needed in making decisions about retaining or destroying files because of the complexity of the legal problems involved.

card file or a folder of certificates authorizing destruction. (See Fig. 10–3.)

INVENTORY & DESTRUCTION AUTHORIZATION REQUEST

Division of Archives and Records Management

REFERENCE: RCW 40.14

PART 1

1. AGENCY TITLE Washington State Patrol	2. REPORTING UNIT Field Force all units
3. RECORDS SERIES TITLE Officers' Notebooks	
4. FUNCTION OF RECORDS SERIES Records of all pertinent data dealing with daily watch of each officer	
5. CONTENT OF RECORDS SERIES Personal notes of each officer - notebook form	

6. ARRANGEMENT OF RECORDS SERIES: ALPHA [ ] (Type) · NUMERIC [ ] (Type) · SUBJECT [ ] (Type) · OTHER (Specify) [X] Chronological

7. RECORDS SIZE: LETTER · LEGAL · CARD · MIXTURE · EDP · OTHER (Specify) Notebook size 5x8

8. VOLUME OF RECORDS 60 FILE DRAWERS ___ CUBIC FEET ___ INCHES	9. INCLUSIVE DATES FROM 1921 TO 1969	10. RATE OF ANNUAL ACCUMULATION ___ FILE DRAWERS 5 CUBIC FEET ___ INCHES	11. PORTION OF RECORD IN STORAGE? (If so, where?) All over 1 year old-with each officer

12. RATE OF REFERENCE TO RECORDS SERIES PORTION 1 YEAR OLD OR LESS daily PER ___ PORTION OVER 1 YEAR OLD 1 PER month	13. RECORDS SERIES DUPLICATED IN WHOLE OR IN PART? (Where?) Copy #1 None Copy #3 ___ Copy #2 ___ Copy #4 ___

14. INFORMATION FROM RECORD SUMMARIZED IN OTHER RECORDS? (If not, enter NONE)
Accident reports, case reports

15. PERMANENT ADMINISTRATIVE, LEGAL OR RESEARCH VALUE OF RECORD [ ] YES [x] NO	16. RECORD ELIGIBLE FOR MICROFILM? [ ] YES [x] NO	17. RECORD ELIGIBLE FOR TRANSFER TO RECORDS CENTER? (If so, when?) [ ] YES [x] NO AFTER ___

18. RECOMMENDED RETENTION PERIOD 5 years	19. SIGNATURE OF PERSON PREPARING REPORT

PART 2

1. RECOMMENDED RETENTION PERIOD (Non-Permanent Records) 5 years	2. TYPE OF RECORD [ ] OFFICIAL PUBLIC RECORD [X] OFFICE FILE & MEMORANDA

3. JUSTIFICATION FOR DESTRUCTION
Of no value for reference or legal purposes after 5 years

4. RECORD PRESERVATION [ ] YES [ ] MICROFILM [x] NO [ ] RELEASE TO ARCHIVES	5. SPECIAL STATUTORY REQUIREMENTS (Other than RCW 40.14) None	6. SIGNATURE OF AGENCY RECORDS OFFICER

PART 3

1. ACTION ON REQUEST [x] APPROVED [ ] APPROVED AS AMENDED [ ] UNAPPROVED	2. AUTHORITY NUMBER 69-932

3. COMMENTS OR AMENDMENTS

FOR THE ATTORNEY GENERAL	FOR THE STATE AUDITOR	STATE ARCHIVIST

GAA-8 (Rev. 9-69)
Return all copies to Archives for distribution.
Distribution: Copy 1 - Archives Copy 2 - Records Officer Copy 3 - Office of Record

Figure 10–3. An inventory and destruction authorization request form (*courtesy Washington State Archives*)

The way records are destroyed depends on their importance. Confidential records may be shredded or chemically pulverized. Special shredders are available as office equipment. Burning is prohibited in some urban areas since it contributes to air pollution. Some companies sell useless records as scrap.

Vital Records

Records can be classified as vital, essential, important, useful, and nonessential. The classification is based on the need for them and whether or not they can be replaced.

Vital. "Vital" means necessary to life. Vital records, therefore, are necessary to the life of a company. The company could not stay in business without them. Vital records are sometimes classified according to the chief operations of a company: sales, financial, engineering, legal, manufacturing, research, product formulas, production data, administration, and property management. An inventory sheet of vital records should contain the following information:

1. Title and description of the record or file.
2. Dates.
3. Location of the records.
4. Name of person in charge.
5. Possible duplicate or source records elsewhere.

Copying equipment makes it possible now to keep facsimile copies of vital records in several locations. Most companies keep several sets.

Essential. The loss of essential records would not put the company out of business, but their replacement would be costly and difficult if they were burned or otherwise destroyed. It is sometimes hard to distinguish between vital and essential papers. Many computer records, especially data processing programs, fall into the "essential" classification.

Important. Sales statistics, budget data, and backup or source data for various types of business reports are *important* papers. They are needed; yet if they are destroyed, they can be replaced with a minimum of effort.

Useful. Records that have historical value may be classified as "useful." That is, such records can be used as a management resource in tracing the development of the company and of its policies. The historical value of records should be approved by someone high in the company.

Protecting Records

If records are worth keeping at all, they are worth protecting. The greatest enemy is fire. Other enemies are dust, water, warfare, and careless handling. Confidential records must also be protected against prying eyes, vandalism, and loss. Every secretary should give some thought to how well the files she handles are protected.

The easiest way to protect records from prying eyes and vandalism is to *lock* them into a safe, file, or desk. Safeguarding them from fires and disasters requires several additional precautions:

1. Storage areas should be equipped with fire extinguishers.
2. Sprinkler systems should be installed.
3. Air ducts should be checked and kept clean.
4. Aisles, corners, and tops of file cabinets should not be cluttered with piles of records.
5. Smoking should be restricted in records storage areas.
6. Copies of essential and vital records should be kept in remote storage.

Remote Storage. Copies of essential and vital records should be kept in several locations, properly safeguarded. Safety deposit boxes are suitable for some, but most businesses need larger remote storage centers. Since it was realized that records possibly could be destroyed by atomic bombs, remote bombproof records centers have been established. A company may rent space in such centers. Some are located in underground caves that have been equipped with humidity controls, stand-by generators, and controlled vault and storage areas. Underground Vaults and Storage, Inc., located in Kansas, is an example of this type of security center. It involves 128 acres, is about 650 feet underground, and its "ceiling" is rock salt, shale, and sandy soil. (See Fig. 10–4.)

Filing Manuals

A filing manual describes files and includes instructions on how to operate them. Every office should have a filing manual of some type, even if it is only a page or two of description kept in a folder. If the office in which you work is small and there is not even a sheet in a folder describing the files, prepare one. Tell what the files contain, how the system of tabs and guides was originally designed, how the charge-out system works, how you cross reference and how the related index (if any) can be used.

Figure 10–4. Underground storage
(*courtesy Underground Vaults and Storage, Inc.*)

> *General Rules*
>
> Each office should have a filing manual which describes types of files that are kept and that explains some of the basic operating practices.
>
> A good filing manual also provides clear instructions on *how to use* the manual.

Manuals have three purposes:

1. To tell how files work;
2. To inform other people about them;
3. To control their operations.

Large companies usually have filing operations manuals that describe types of files, their purposes, filing policies and standard practices, subject classifications, and such filing operations as cross referencing, charging out records, disposition schedules, and general files handling. The introduction of one company's filing manual (a 228-page manual) stated the following purposes:

1. Provide a definite source of instruction and guidance for those responsible for processing and filing company records.
2. Set forth procedures to systematize and improve the maintenance of current files used to conduct daily business throughout the company.
3. Help train new personnel in filing procedures.
4. Obtain maximum results from all filing efforts in the company.

Secretaries should have copies of company filing manuals and should read them carefully. One company put the following jingle on the cover of its filing manual:

> Some folks file and cannot find.
> Let's not be the "can't find" kind.
> Read this manual — to the letter
> And you'll find you're filing better.[3]

Secretaries should not be timid about making suggestions for additions or changes that they think are necessary. A secretary's desire to help is respected if she offers her suggestions in the right spirit.

General Rule

Keep those concerned with your files informed. Consult with them. Communicate with them about bottlenecks and improvements. Check classification systems and ideas for improvement with them.

General Procedures

The ability to find items in a file reflects not only the type of system and equipment used, but the care with which the file is maintained as well. Keep the filing up to date. File at a regular time each day. Do not let papers accumulate outside the files. Keep them moving back to the files. Keep careful charge-out records. Set limits on how long records can be out of the files, even if the limitation is only tentative and has to be changed later. Check "due dates" on your charge-out tickets and follow up items that have not been returned,

---

[3] Lever Brothers File Manual.

even if they have been issued to the president's office. Use reminder systems that work so that you do not have to load your memory with a lot of details. *Make your files work for you.*

General Rules

When contents are removed from files, a charge-out marker should be inserted.

Some type of tickler or reminder system should be used to help recall materials removed from files.

A Guide to Good Filing Procedure

1. Stop filing that which should be destroyed.
2. Spot check material in the file against material to be filed.
3. Charge out records and recharge them if they are transferred to another person.
4. Stop people who don't trust central files from starting their own private files.
5. Have a retention setup.
6. Maintain proper primary index frequency.
7. Be neat always.
8. Keep people from circumventing proper return-to-file procedures.
9. Presort.
10. Plan indexing for expansion and to reduce misfiles.
11. Avoid overloading equipment and folders.
12. Be sure your filing staff is well trained.
13. Know the fundamentals of filing.
14. Be sure you're using filing supplies correctly.
15. Establish a central control of records management. Provide for the operation of centralized and decentralized records for all offices under one authority and one responsibility.
16. Study your file room layout to be sure it's properly designed for the job you have to do.
17. Review your forms design to be sure they are not unnecessarily complicating in-file reading of documents.

18. Learn your company's paper handling costs. You may find that
     they're substantial enough so that you should consult a filing
     systems expert.

Wherever possible, use simplified paper-handling practices. That is,
look for chances to eliminate unnecessary work. For example, write
answers directly on routine request letters, returning the "nota-
tioned" letters to the sender. Keep unnecessary items out of the files.
Mark disposition dates on short-lived items so they will be thrown
away when they have served their purpose and will not clutter the
files. Use good housekeeping practices such as keeping papers in a
folder tamped down and even. Such practices improve the overall
efficiency as well as appearance of your filing systems.

Review Questions

1. What are transfer records?
2. What is the perpetual transfer method?
3. What is the periodic transfer method?
4. What is a vital record?
5. Against what do filed records need to be protected?
6. Describe three ways to protect records.
7. What is a retention schedule?
8. Why are retention schedules desirable?
9. Who should develop a retention schedule for files maintained by
    a secretary?
10. Why are filing manuals important?
11. What should a filing manual contain?

Review Exercises

Review Exercise 1

    a. Find a dictionary definition for the following words.
    b. Type the definitions neatly and use each item in an
       office work-oriented sentence.
    c. Hand the exercise to the instructor for checking.

    1. Vital Records   4. Retention Schedule
    2. Facsimile   5. Destruction Schedule
    3. Safeguard   6. Operating Manual

Review Exercise 2

a. Prepare an appropriate answer "sheet" on a 5″ by 3″ card. Give it a title.

b. Indicate by writing the letter name (*a, b, . . .*) of the definition that best defines each word in the first column.

c. Hand the exercise to the instructor for checking.

Word	*Definition*
1. Filing _____	a. A concentration of records often maintained by file specialists.
2. Vital Record _____	
3. Periodic Transfer _____	
4. Central File _____	
5. Retention Schedule _____	b. Identifiable, standardized items, or pieces of information.
6. Out guide _____	
	c. The storage of data and information.
	d. The movement at stated intervals, at a definite time, of inactive files out of active files.
	e. A record or tracer that is left when a file item is removed.
	f. An item that is necessary to the life or continuity of a company.
	g. A list of things to keep in company archives.

Projects

Project 1. *Recommendations*

Purpose: The goals of this project are to:

1. acquaint you with the organization of a filing operations manual;

2. help you realize the content and organization of a filing manual.

Instructions:

1. Make a list of some of the topics you would cover in a filing operations manual if you prepared one for this situation.
2. Take *one* of the following situations. Assume you work for —
    a. A university professor of business education who specializes primarily in teaching improved office procedures.
    b. A medical doctor who specializes in heart diseases.
    c. An office manager who is in charge of personnel, purchasing office supplies and equipment, and of the central filing, stenographic, mailing, and duplicating services of the company. He has already prepared an office manual that has sections about each of the office services. You help him keep the manual up to date and see that it is issued to those who need it.
3. Alphabetize and sectionalize (with subheadings) the "Table of Contents" you have just prepared.
4. Type the list. Give it a heading.
5. Hand the project to the instructor for checking.

11

Microfilm and Automated Filing Systems

Microfilm

Vital and important records are often microfilmed. Microfilming is the process of photographing records and reducing the film copy to a miniature size. Microfilm can save 95 to 98 percent of the space needed for storing original records. An example of extreme miniaturization is shown in Fig. 11-1.

Microfilm comes in two sizes: 16 and 35 millimeter. A 100-foot reel of 16-mm film will store 8,000 images of bank checks or about 2500 images of letter-sized documents. The reel can be stored in a 4" x 4" x 1" box. If a double row of images is made, 22,000 check images can be put on a 100-foot reel. This gives some idea of the space that can be conserved when microfilming is used. Because of this consolidation feature, microfilm can make large quantities of records quickly accessible. Viewing equipment spins through reels of microfilm in seconds. Microfilm is even a part of computer installations. A system called COM (Computer Output Microfilm) produces microfilm of computer printouts at thousands of frames a minute.

Microfilming is particularly applicable for files of engineering drawings that are too large and bulky for easy handling. It is also useful for miniaturizing copies of newspapers, books, and other library materials. In companies where reports or other data are sent to branch offices, shipping microfilm in lieu of paper copies can result in significant savings. Microfilm readers are easy to use. Equipment is also available which quickly makes paper copies of microfilm images when they are needed. This equipment is found in many offices. Although microfilming has many advantages, it is important that the costs of microfilming be compared to the savings in each situation.

The material to be microfilmed may require special preparation due to variable sizes and legibility. Such factors as serviceability for reference, the cost of printouts, the number of readers and/or printers required, and the retention time for the paper copies need to be considered before a microfilming program is established.

Figure 11-1. Microfilm of the Holy Bible containing 1,245 pgs.
(courtesy NCR)

Aperture Cards. Not all microfilm is stored in reels. An aperture card combines a microfilm with a punched card. (See Fig. 11-2.) In a small filing system, aperture cards can be kept like ordinary file cards and hunted manually. They are, of course, most useful when automatic equipment for reading and sorting punched cards is available.

Aperture cards are used for filing and retrieving maps, property-title records, real estate records, patents, medical records, and engineering and architectural drawings.

Microfiche. "Fiche" is a French word that means *card.* It is pronounced *feesh.* Microfiche, therefore, is a card of microfilm. (See Fig. 11-3.) *Sheets* of microfilm are also called microfiche. A microfiche sheet (or card) can hold microfilms of sixty or so pages. Micro-

Figure 11-2. An aperture card carries mounted microfilm
(courtesy 3M Company)

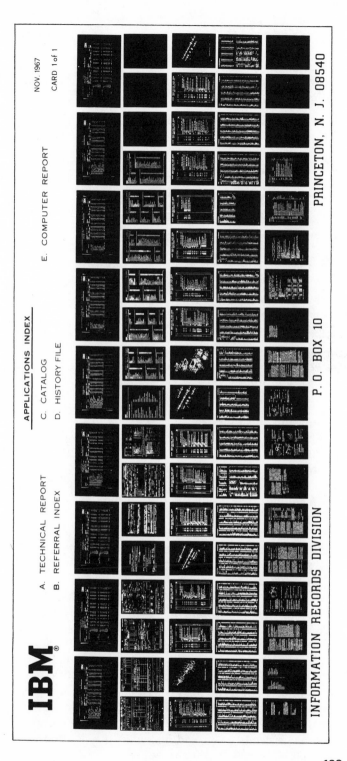

Figure 11-3. Microfiche
(courtesy IBM)

fiche can be indexed with captions visible to the naked eye so that
they can be handled like regular cards.

Acetate Jacket Cards. Acetate jacket cards hold loose microfilm
chips or short strips. They provide filing flexibility because chips can
be added, taken out, or changed in sequence. (See Fig. 11–4.)

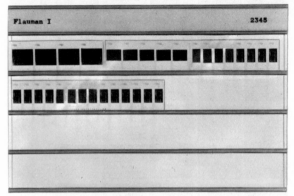

Figure 11–4. Acetate jacket compartmentalized by ribs
of extruded cellulose acetate
(*courtesy NB Jackets Corp.*)

Automation and Filing

For some time men have envisioned automating the handling of
business information, thus freeing office employees from many routine paperhandling tasks. *Automatic* data processing involves computers and auxiliary machines that input and output data and
instructions for computers and store them for future use. Filing is
only one phase of data processing — the storage phase. Information
is stored on punched cards, punched or magnetic tape, disks, laser
beams, or as mark-sensed dots (which some types of computers can
read) on various card forms.

When computers were first introduced, it was thought that
computer-oriented data storage equipment would entirely replace
manual filing. The computer age is now about twenty years old, and
manual filing has not been wiped out yet — nor is it likely to be.
There will always be the need for paper copies of documents that
people can handle, carry about with them, and study at their convenience. To use computer files, the boss has to be hooked up with
computer equipment. He can, of course, use a television-type screen
(called a CRT — cathode ray tube) in his office to question computerized files whenever he needs to, providing he has the right equipment. He can also make changes in information while it is projected
on his CRT screen with a device called a "light" pencil. Or he can

communicate directly with the computer via a typewriter-like key-board that is part of a CRT installation. However, as yet, he cannot carry these "files" in his car or take parts of them home to study.

There will also always be some personal files, particularly files of correspondence that a manager will keep in his office. A secretary, therefore, cannot write filing off her list of duties. She will, at least for the foreseeable future, be involved with filing of the type discussed in this Workbook. Increasingly, however, she undoubtedly will work with computerized printouts of information, and she even may be involved in keying-in inquiries or instructions on her boss's CRT computer hookup. As small businesses rent more computer time and go on-line to central service computer installations, before long even the small insurance and real estate office will probably have some of its files of data computerized. For these reasons, well-qualified secretaries need to know something about computer "files."

Tape Storage

Magnetic tape, the same width as that used in tape recorders, is a popular computer data storage device for several reasons:

1. Since tape is a continuous strip, it can be processed by computer readers faster than punched cards. About a thousand digits of data can be packed on an inch of tape and the tape moves over reading heads at hundreds of inches a second.
2. The information is stored on magnetic tape in the form of magnetic dots not visible to the human eye. The dots are "sensed" by the computer readers.
3. Tape retains the stored dots without deterioration for a very long time.

Tape libraries (see Fig. 11–5) are common sights in computer centers. Billions of digits of data and hundreds of instructions are *filed* on reels of tape. The reels are sometimes in metal containers to keep them free from dust.

Punched *paper* tape, the type used in some accounting machines for billing, can also send data to computers. The Flexowriter (type-writer) as well as automatic typewriters produce and use punched tape. These tapes are sometimes used by secretaries who work with bookkeeping machines and automatic typewriters. They can be stored as illustrated in Figs. 11–6 and 11–7.

Figure 11-5. A tape library in a computer center
(*courtesy The Wright Line*)

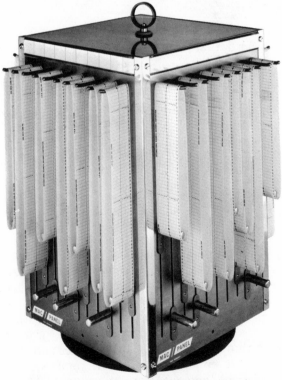

Figure 11-6. A tape rack with adjustable pins
(*courtesy MacPanel Co.*)

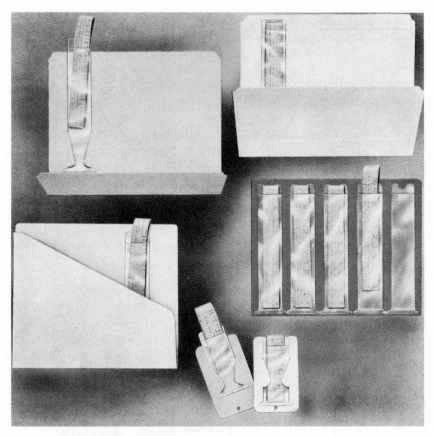

Figure 11-7. Tape files

Disk Packs

A computer disk pack is a stack of "platters," usually in piles of six, similar to those used for music and played by disk jockeys. Magnetic disk packs are a new way to "file" computer data. Magnetic specks of data are stored on both sides of the platters, and playing heads can reach any location on either side of a disk merely by being given the proper command (location "address") by a computer program. This type of data access has advantages over magnetic tapes. On tape, the information is strung out in strips dozens of feet long. To locate a particular piece of information may mean whirling through an entire length of tape. This is not so with the disk packs; if one programs in the address via the computer program, the reading head will move directly to that location on the disk.

Disk packs, although invented only a few years ago, are widely used. A pack containing thousands of digits of data can be lifted in and out of a reading unit as easily as a new record can be put on a phonograph. Because of their size, storing disk packs is a problem. So far, they are stored primarily in partitions on shelves. Highly confidential data may, of course, need to be stored in a vault.

Magnetic Cards

Computer readers can also input information from *cards* that have been prepared with magnetic ink. (See Fig. 11–8.) Cards prepared in this way are called mark-sensed cards and the procedure is generally referred to as Magnetic Character Recognition (MCR). The marks must be made with special electrographic pencils or ink. Usually the process involves having equipment read the MCR cards and automatically convert the information to punched cards or magnetic tape.

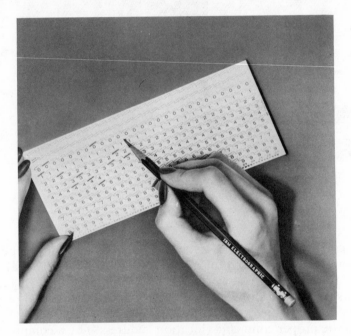

Figure 11–8. IBM mark-sensed card
(*courtesy IBM*)

MCR cards have a special advantage. They can be marked away from the office. For example, assume that the man who reads home water meters marks a properly designed card while reading your meter. The card is then ready for automatic processing, bypassing manual typing, sorting, or key-punching. The cards may be filed in batches the same as punched cards. Since they can be sorted automatically, they do not need guides.

Edge-punched Cards

A unique manual method of filing and retrieving data on cards is the edge-punched card system. In this system the cards have holes around the outer edge in a coded sequence; numbers and word descriptors can be symbolized by notching out the appropriate holes. Several companies design and install these systems; among the well-known trade names are McBee Key Sort, E-Z Sort, and Flexisort. An old idea, the edge-punched card system is still one of the easiest and simplest ways to record and sort certain types of information. (See Figs. 11–9 and 11–10.)

Figure 11–9. Edge-punched cards being needled
(*courtesy Royal McBee Corporation*)

To code edge-punched cards, one punches out the appropriately classified hole so that it becomes an open notch. Holes can be notched manually or mechanically. When a "needle" (like an ice pick) is inserted in holes in the desired location in a batch of cards, those which have been notched will drop out because the hole has been opened, while the other cards will be suspended on the needle. Because of this quick sorting feature, cards can be stored in random sequence. The edge-punched card system is ideal for systems under 10,000 cards.

Beyond that, "needling" active card files becomes a physical burden and automatic punched card systems should be used.

The arrangement of information on an edge-punched card differs from user to user. The following code, however, is basic. When coding notched cards, four digits (7, 4, 2, 1) are used:

Hundreds	Tens	Units
0 0 0 0	0 0 0 0	0 0 0 0
0 0 0 0	0 0 0 0	0 0 0 0
7 4 2 1	7 4 2 1	7 4 2 1

(Part of a Card)

When a single row of holes is used around the edge of a card, numbers can be combined (and grooved) to make any digit from one to nine. Ciphers are not notched. If you were coding $195, you would notch the first row of holes as follows:

Hundreds	Tens	Units
0 0 0 ●	● 0 ● 0	0 ● 0 ●

Edge-punched cards might be used in a real estate office. When a customer calls a realtor, he usually has in mind a particular type of property: price range, number of bedrooms, bathrooms, and garages, hardwood floors or carpeting, ranch style or colonial, fireplaces, yard, fruit trees, and so on. The card used by the realtor can contain a picture of the property (see Fig. 11–10) and provide space for written

Figure 11–10. An edge-punched card with picture of a piece of real estate (*courtesy Royal McBee Corporation*)

information about terms, associated realtors, and so on. Around the edge are the holes for classifications that describe the property, properly notched for each piece. In a few minutes of needling, hundreds of cards can be searched and those that most nearly describe property in which the customer is interested will be readily available.

Punched Cards

Punched cards (see Figs. 11–11 and 11–12) are often called *unit records*. Until magnetic tape became popular, punched cards were the primary way of storing data for computers. Punched cards are still used widely, and companies that have computer installations have many files of them.

Each card is punched and read as a unit so that each transaction – for example, an inventory item in stock is added to – is "filed" on a separate card. The amount of data recorded on one card is restricted by the size and design of the card. This is no problem, though, because if more space is needed, the information is merely continued to another card. Sequence among related cards is easy to maintain by numbering them.

The "units" of information stored on punched cards can be meshed together automatically in any desired order. For example, if we want to integrate information contained on hundreds of cards, we process them automatically to get printed lists of such things as items in stock, items out of stock, items by price and so on.

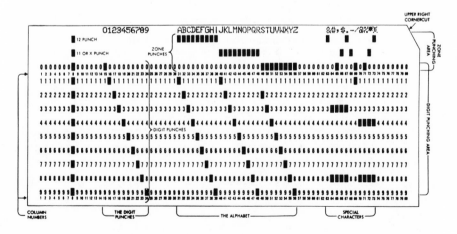

Figure 11–11. An IBM punched card
(*courtesy IBM*)

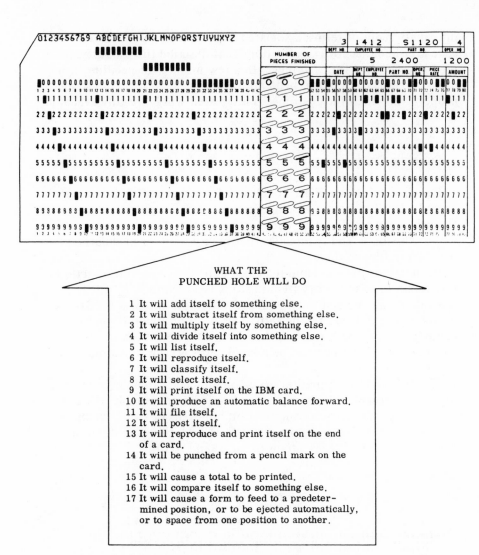

Figure 11-12. What a punched card will do
(*courtesy IBM*)

Punched cards are filed in traditional vertical file drawers or boxes (see Fig. 11-14), but the problem of classification that we have with manual card files does not exist. Punched cards do not need to be filed in any special sequence because the mechanical equipment sorts them. For this reason, punched cards are usually filed in random batches.

Figure 11-13. Machine print-out reports neatly filed
(*courtesy The Wright Line*)

Crayon or pen and ink comments do not in any way interfere with the mechanical processing of punched cards. They may, therefore, be marked for manual accessing, although they rarely are. If and when they are, some visual indexing is needed. Guide cards should be used, with classification tabs standing above the regular height of the cards so that they can be read easily. Color coding can also be used. It is helpful to write with a marking pencil the number or date of the first and last card on a label for the front of the drawer or across the top of a batch of cards. (When the cards are resorted, the numbers must be changed.) Marking cards in this way helps to find batches of them quickly.

Machine Forms

Most of the printout from computers is on continuous sheets of manifold paper (see Fig. 11-13), and they are produced so fast by computers (more than a thousand lines a minute) that filing the printouts is a problem. What is more, the printouts are bulky.

**Figure 11-14. A metal file-drawer for tab cards with
compression holders and front labels**
(*courtesy National Blank Book Co., Inc.*)

Retention schedules are needed for them because they accumulate
so fast. So far, open-shelf files work best for machine form printouts.
They are filed flat and the file sections are labeled. In maintaining the
files, consider such housekeeping factors as dust, fire protection, and
safeguarding confidential reports.

Review Questions

1. What is an aperture card? What does it "file"?
2. What is a microfiche? What kind of information does it file?
3. How does microfilming affect filing?
4. What new types of "files" has automatic data processing introduced?
5. How is automatic data processing affecting filing? Give an
   example.

6. How is automatic data processing affecting the files a secretary handles? Give an example.
7. Why is the classification of punched card files not a problem?
8. Why is magnetic tape replacing punched cards?
9. Why are magnetic disks being used more and more?
10. What is a *marginal* punched card filing system? How does the system work?
11. What is magnetic character recognition (MCR)? How are MCR cards filed?
12. What is CRT? How is it used?
13. How can an employer sit in his office and at the same time communicate with "files" stored in a computer?
14. How is magnetic tape stored? How is punched paper stored?

Review Exercises

Review Exercise 1

a. Find dictionary definitions for the following words.
b. Type the definitions neatly and use each term in a sentence.
c. Hand the exercise to the instructor for checking.

1. Microfilm
2. Microfiche
3. Aperture Card
4. Electronic Data Processing
5. Automatic Data Processing

6. Magnetic Tape
7. Disk Packs
8. Magnetic Character Recognition
9. Punched Cards

Review Exercise 2

a. Prepare an appropriate answer sheet for the following true-false, multiple-choice, and completion statements.
b. Indicate true-false answers with a *T* or an *F*.
c. Read each item carefully and check the answer in the chapter, if you need to.
d. Submit the completed exercise to the instructor for checking.

True or False?

1. Microfilming reduces the copy to a miniature size.
2. All microfilm is stored in reels of tape.
3. The word *microfiche* means small card.
4. Computers are replacing manual files.
5. Because computers are replacing manual filing, a secretary can write filing off her list of duties.
6. The boss can consult a computer file via a CRT.
7. Punched paper tape is a primary way to feed data into a computer.
8. Disk packs are replacing punched paper tape as a computer file.
9. MCR filed data can be read automatically.
10. Edge-punched cards can be processed by computers.

Multiple Choice (Use the letter a, b, or c to indicate the correct answer.)

1. Which of the following statements is least true about computer files?
   a. Punched paper tape is a primary computer "file."
   b. Punched cards make satisfactory computer data "files."
   c. Computers are having an impact on manual filing. _____
2. Which of the following statements is true about computer files?
   a. Punched cards can be signaled and arranged back of file guides.
   b. Punched cards store dozens of units of information per card.
   c. Disk packs are too bulky for computer use. _____
3. Which one of the following statements best describes a computer *card* file?
   a. The card can be read by a machine.
   b. Information is punched as holes.
   c. A unit of information is recorded via holes. _____
4. Which one of the following statements describes a computer filing problem?
   a. Punched cards are not classified.

b. Computers produce printed reports at hundreds of lines a minute.

c. Information stored on magnetic tapes is in a continuous strip. _____

Completion Statements. (Supply the word that best completes the following statements.)

1. Most of the computer printouts are on continuous sheets of _____ paper.

2. The amount of data recorded on one punched card is restricted by the _____ and _____ of the card.

3. Each punched card is punched and read as a _____ .

4. A well-known trade name for an edge-punched card is _____ .

5. Filing disk packs is a problem because of their _____ .

6. Tape libraries are common sights in _____ .

Projects

Project 1. *Collecting Information about Computer Files*

Purpose: The goals of this project are to:

1. update your knowledge about computer files;
2. help your class collect literature and illustrations about computer files;
3. give you experience in creating a filing system for illustrative information.

Materials: Unless the instructor wants to use school letterhead, you will need several sheets of plain white stationery, envelopes, and postage stamps.

Instructions:

1. Consult the list of filing supply manufacturers in Appendix B of this Workbook and select two firms to which

you will write asking for illustrative materials about *computer files.*

2. Prepare a draft of the letter asking the education departments of the companies you've selected for illustrative materials. Have the draft approved by the instructor.

3. After the draft of the letter is approved by the instructor, write the two letters, check them carefully for errors, sign the letters, address the envelopes, stamp the letters, and mail them. What return address did you give?

4. Anticipate the type of materials that you and other students will accumulate in this way. Prepare a list of ten subject topics and alphabetize them. What primary guides do you recommend?

5. Sketch the filing system as you visualize it.

6. Submit the sketch and the carbon copies of your letters to the instructor. Consider preparing a bulletin board display when the materials come.

Project 2. *Overall Review Quiz*

Purpose:

a. to review entire Workbook

b. to help you crystallize some of your technical knowledge about filing and records management.

Instructions:

1. Prepare an appropriate answer sheet. Use the letter *a, b, c,* or *d* to indicate the correct answer.

2. Write *why* you think the answer is correct.

3. Put your name and the date in the upper right corner of the sheet, and hand it to the instructor for grading.

1. All but which one of the following are advantages of microfilming records?

a. Allows optimal use of space.

b. Makes individual, original documents easily accessible.

c. Insures accuracy because it provides photographic duplicates.

d. Safeguards vital records.

Why?

2. All but which one of the following statements describes a characteristic of a filing system?
   a. Each collects items that are organized into subdivisions.
   b. Each has a miscellaneous section.
   c. Each uses color coding.
   d. Each may include special guides and subdivisions.
   Why?

3. The mental process by which the name, subject, or other caption in a filing system is determined is called
   a. systematizing
   b. indexing
   c. coding
   d. sorting
   Why?

4. Probably the best filing system for a large manufacturing company to use for maintaining employee histories is
   a. numeric
   b. subject
   c. alphabetic
   d. subject
   Why?

5. In an active card file, a guide should be used for every
   a. 20 cards
   b. 30 cards
   c. 40 cards
   d. 50 cards
   Why?

6. The most common alphabetic pattern in alphabetizing individual name filing systems is
   a. word by word
   b. name by name
   c. unit by unit
   d. letter by letter
   Why?

7. An alphabetic filing system that uses color to speed up the location of items is called
   a. Colorama
   b. Soundex
   c. Triple-Check Automatic Check
   d. Variadex
   Why?

8. In drawer files, a guide should be used for about every
   a. 8 folders
   b. 10 folders
   c. 12 folders
   d. 14 folders
   Why?

9. In numeric filing, the system that divides the numbers into separate groups of digits and then considers the group on the right
   as the *primary* classification is
   a. alpha-numeric
   b. decimal-numeric
   c. duplex-numeric
   d. terminal-digit
   Why?

10. A machine that projects a magnification of a microfilm onto a
    viewing screen is called a
    a. microfiche
    b. reader
    c. blowup
    d. microrecord
    Why?

11. On the average, the percent of business records that should be
    kept permanently is
    a. 10%
    b. 15%
    c. 20%
    d. 35%
    Why?

12. A filing system that helps to insure necessary follow-up action
    at a specific time is a
    a. date folder
    b. tickler file
    c. daily file
    d. back-up file
    Why?

13. The transfer method, where only inactive materials are trans-
    ferred at regular intervals, is called
    a. perpetual
    b. one-period
    c. two-period
    d. maximum-minimum period
    Why?

14. The least important thing to consider when creating an office filing system is which one of the following:
    a. the supplies available
    b. who needs the materials
    c. how often the records are used
    d. what disposition will be made of the records
    Why?

15. If you can't remember the correct descriptor for a subject file, you would consult which one of the following:
    a. a filing manual
    b. a relative index
    c. a fellow employee
    d. the department head
    Why?

A

Glossary

ABBREVIATION — A shortened form of a word. In indexing, an abbreviation is considered as though it were spelled in full. (2)*

ACETATE JACKET — A card form that holds portions of film strips or microfilm so that they are visible under a plastic coating. (11)

ACTIVE RECORDS — Records that are referred to relatively often and which should be readily accessible in the office area. They are sometimes called "current" records. (3)

ALPHABETIC FILING — Any system that arranges names or topics according to the sequence of letters in the alphabet. (2)

ALPHABETIZE — To arrange in the prescribed sequence according to the letters of the alphabet. (2)

ALPHA-NUMERIC — Systems made up of combinations of letters and numbers. (7)

AMERICAN RECORDS MANAGEMENT ASSOCIATION — A national group interested in the study of efficient records making and records keeping. It conducts research in standardized alphabetical filing, shelf-filing methods and equipment, machine-processed data control, and retention practices. (2)

APERTURE CARD — A punched or notched card with a single microfilm mounted in the center right-hand side. It may be referred to as a point-of-use card. Aperture cards can be manipulated automatically or needled (edge-notched cards). (11)

*Numbers after glossary entries refer to the chapter in which the item is introduced.

ARCHIVE – A collection of items of historical significance to a company. (10)

AUTOMATION – An automatic procedure or device replacing human effort and employing feedback of information so that it may be self-correcting. Sometimes used to describe extensive mechanization in a factory or office. (11)

AUXILIARY EQUIPMENT – Supporting or supplementary equipment; for example, a sorter, a file stool, or a filing shelf. (5)

BINDER – A semi-permanent holder of papers. (5)

BLOW-UP – The picture that is projected on a screen when microfilm is put into a viewer. (11)

CABINET – A container with drawers for filing records. (5)

CAPTION – A heading, title, or subtitle under which records are filed. It is usually found on the tab of a file folder. (4)

CARD DESIGN – The arrangement of constant items and lines on a card form. (9)

CARD FILING – The process of listing and storing information on cards. Two types of card files are: visible and vertical. (9)

CARD STRIPS – Narrow strips of paper used for visible files of one- or two-line items. (9)

CARD UNIT – A single document or form upon which information may be accumulated. (9)

CARRIER FOLDER – A folder used to transport records from the files to wherever they are needed. This folder is made of a heavy material and usually of a specific color. (5)

CENTRAL FILE – A concentration of records often maintained by file specialists. It may be departmental or company-wide. (10)

CHARACTER SENSING – Mechanical reading of symbols or marks made with special ink or pencil. (11)

CHARGE-OUT – A control procedure for locating records that have been removed from files. Its function is to ensure that records removed from the files will be returned. (3)

CHARGE-OUT CARD – A card inserted in the file in place of loaned material that identifies and indicates the location of the material. Also called the file-out card. (9)

CHIPS – Single frames of microfilm that are cut and coded for quick access and identification by automatic equipment. (11)

CHRONOLOGIC FILE – A numeric file in which items are filed by date. (7)

CLASSIFICATION PLAN — A predetermined arrangement of the contents of a file according to key items and relationships. It identifies, groups, standardizes, and codifies information into a cohesive whole. (1)

CLASSIFYING — The act of determining by analysis the group under which records are to be filed or cross referenced under an established plan.

CODING — The marking of materials with captions under which they will be stored. (3)

COMPOUND NAME — A designation composed of two or more words. (2)

COMPRESSOR — That part of a follow block that presses standing folders together in a file drawer when they are not in use. (5) See "Follow Block."

CORRESPONDENCE — Records representing formal communications between two or more parties by letter, telegram, memorandum, and the like.

CREATIVITY — Ability to be productive or inventive. (4)

CROSS FILE — The practice of filing vertically across the width rather than the length of a file drawer. (5)

CROSS-FILING — The putting of duplicates of a record in as many places as necessary. (3)

CROSS REFERENCE — A notation in a file telling that a record is stored elsewhere; it gives the reference. (3)

CUT — The size of the tab on a folder, which is usually expressed as a dimension. For example, a one-third cut means that the cut takes up one third of the back flap of the folder. (5)

DATA PROCESSING — Any method by which facts are collected, classified, stored, and retrieved. (11)

DECIMAL-NUMERIC — A filing classification system in which file headings are numbers. The test of a good decimal-numeric classification is the logic of its sequence of classification. The numbering provides a means of holding the overall classification pattern together. (7)

DEPARTMENTAL FILES — Files in which the records of one department are kept in that one department, or kept separately from the records of other departments.

DESTRUCTION SCHEDULE — A listing of dates on which records are to be destroyed. (10) See "Retention Schedule."

DICTIONARY PATTERN – An arrangement of items in strict alphabetical sequence regardless of relationships. (4)

DIE CUT – A folder that has been shaped by a cutting mold. (5)

DIRECT FILING SYSTEM – A filing plan whereby information or material can be located without consulting an intermediary source of reference. (7) See "Indirect Filing System."

DISPOSING, DISPOSITION – Destroying or eliminating records that are no longer needed. (10)

DISPOSITION SCHEDULE – A plan for the preservation and orderly disposition of records; an itemized list of records specifying disposition actions to be taken at stated intervals. (10)

DIVIDER – Generally a metal plate or stiff guide designed to keep files from sagging. (5)

DOCUMENTS – Any items printed or written that are relied upon to record or prove something. (3)

DRAWER FILE – An accumulation of records (usually stored on edge) in a box-type file that can be drawn out and then pushed back into place. Records are placed in drawer files face front, the top edge of the document to the left, with most recent data on top. (3)

EDGE-NOTCHED CARDS – File cards containing a border of holes that may be notched to indicate (code) items of information. Also called "edge-punched cards." (9)

ELECTRONIC, ELECTRIC – Electronic equipment is electrical, but electric equipment is not necessarily electronic. Electrical equipment may have physically moving parts; in electronic equipment, that which moves is an electrical impulse. (11)

ELECTRONIC DATA PROCESSING (EDP) – Storing and manipulating information through electronic computer equipment. (11)

ELECTRONIC EQUIPMENT – Devices that use electric circuitry to perform data-processing operations such as arithmetic. Impulses are directed from transistor tubes that have no physically moving parts. (11)

ENCYCLOPEDIC PATTERN – Information grouped first under key headings as to content, then subtopics that are alphabetized under key headings. An example of the encyclopedic pattern is the Yellow Pages in a telephone directory, which groups businesses as to type and then alphabetizes them within each type. (4)

ESSENTIAL RECORDS – Less important records than vital ones, but still costly and difficult to reconstruct if destroyed. (10) See "Vital Records."

FACSIMILE — An exact photographic duplicate. (11)

FANFOLD — That part of a folder that is pleated for expansion. (5)

FILE — Papers or data that have been accumulated about a subject or matter of business. Also, a large collection of records representing the business of an organization. (1)

FILE INDEX — An ordered list of items designating where a record is within a filing system. (3)

FILE REQUISITIONS — Requests for filed material generally written on a special form. A requisition form might also be used as a charge-out. (3) See "Charge-Out."

FILES — Containers for storing records: folders, cabinets, shelves, and boxes. (1)

FILING — The process of classifying and storing records so that they may be found when needed. (1)

FILING RULES — "Standards or guides" for consistency. They cut to a minimum filing that might result from personal choice or inexperience. (2)

FILING SYSTEM — A plan for organizing records so that they can be found when needed. There are two basic filing systems: alphabetic and numeric. (1)

FILING UNIT — An item of information. It can be the trade name of a company, the last name of an individual, a compound or coined word, a compound geographical name, a title, or even a number. (2) See "Unit Records."

FINDING — Locating a record that has been stored in the files. (1)

FOLDER — A piece of paper folded so that materials can be stored in it. (5)

FOLLOW BLOCK — The adjustable device at the back of a drawer that holds files upright and permits expansion within the drawer. (5) See "Compressor."

FOLLOW-UP — Checking to see that materials taken from files are returned or that items requiring later attention are tickled so that they will be called up at the appropriate time.

FOLLOW-UP FILE — A file, usually chronological, that calls attention to charged-out records that are overdue or to a job that needs to be done on a certain date. (10)

FORM — A printed record with blank spaces for insertion of variable data.

GEOGRAPHIC FILING — Classifying information alphabetically by countries, states, districts, regions, cities, or towns. (8)

GIVEN NAME — An individual's first name. (2)

GUIDE – A file separator of durable composition that signals various classifications. It also serves to keep folders from sagging. (5)

HYPHENATED NAME – An individual or organization name that contains words connected by a hyphen. A hyphenated surname is considered as one unit for indexing. (2)

INACTIVE RECORDS – Records that are referred to relatively seldom and that are often stored. They are sometimes called "non-current" or "dead" records.

INDEX – An ordered list (usually alphabetical) of items (names, key words, or topics) within a body of information. (3)

INDEXING – Choosing the caption under which a record is to be filed. (3)

INDEXING ARRANGEMENT – The order in which units of a name are marked for filing; for example, surname first, then given name. (3)

INDIRECT FILING SYSTEM – A system requiring reference to some source of information before locating the desired materials; that is, one cannot go directly to the material. (7)

INDIVIDUAL FOLDER – A folder for the records of one correspondent. (4)

INFORMATION MAINTENANCE – Keeping data in a state of repair and usability. (10)

INFORMATION PROCESSING – The manipulation of data through a series of changes in order to put it into a new form for use. (11)

INFORMATION RETRIEVAL – Recalling and repossessing data at any time it is needed. (1)

INPUT – The point at which information is fed into a system. (11)

INSPECTING – Examining records for filing release marks. (3)

INTEGRATED DATA-PROCESSING (IDP) – Coordinating information among the various units involved: files, work stations, and machines. (11)

KRAFT – A type and quality of paper; usually brown and heavy weight. (5)

LABEL – A sticker for the tab of a guide or folder on which the caption appears. (5)

LAMINATING SYNTHETIC – A man-made substance that coats and preserves paper documents. (5)

MAGNETIC CARDS – Cards on which information can be stored in magnetic fields. (11)

MAGNETIC INK – Ink containing an iron ingredient so that it can be read automatically. (11)

MAGNETIC TAPE – Special foil or plastic tape used for data storage for computer systems. Data are "written" onto the tape in a pattern of magnetized dots that the computer can read. Eight hundred to a thousand "dots" can be packed onto an inch of tape. (11) See "Magnetic Cards."

MANIFOLD FORMS – Continuous forms perforated at folds for easy separation. (11)

MANILA – A type of paper, usually off-white color, of durable composition. (5)

MANUAL (policy, administrative, or operational) – A reference book. (10)

MAP-AND-TACK FILE – A geographic information system with content classification represented by pins or tacks stuck into a map. Color coding may be used. (8)

MARK SENSING – The act of marking cards with lead that contains a "metal" ingredient so that they can be read automatically by special machines. (11)

MECHANIZATION – The replacement of human effort with machine effort. (11)

MICROFICHE – The sheet version of microfilm. Selected groups of related photographs are put onto a single sheet protected by an acetate cover. (11)

MICROFILMING – Photographing records in reduced size on film. (11)

MICRORECORD – A record that has been preserved in microfilm. (11)

MISCELLANEOUS FOLDER – Folders holding records for a variety of correspondents or subjects. There should be at least five records for an individual folder. (4)

MOBILE FILE – Any file that is easily transported. (5)

NONSIGNIFICANT NUMBERS – Numbers that do not have a subject matter meaning. (7)

NONVERIFIABLE NAMES – Names for which the exact spelling cannot always be established. (4)

NUMERIC FILING — Filing records, correspondence, or cards by number. (7)

OUT FOLDER — A folder for storing records when the regular folder is out of the files. An out folder gives the name of the person borrowing the records. (3)

OUT GUIDE — Indicates that a folder has been taken from the files. (10)

OUTPUT — The information that comes out of a data-processing system. It is the opposite of input. (11)

PHONETIC SYSTEMS — Arrangement of items according to pronunciation. (4)

POINT (measure of thickness) — A unit of measurement for identifying the thickness of paper. (5)

POSITION (1st, 2nd) — The placement of tabs along the top of a folder or guide. (5)

POSTED CARD RECORD — A card to which information is recorded periodically. (9)

PREFABRICATED SYSTEMS — A set of guides and folders designed before the facts and then adapted to the changing conditions of a particular situation. Opposite of tailor-made systems. Also called "commercial" systems. (4) See "System."

PRESSBOARD — Used for guides identified by stiffness and thickness. (5) See "Kraft" and "Manila."

PRIMARY GUIDE — The first and main guide for a section of filed records. (4)

PUNCHED CARDS — Cards with holes punched in them that translate our language into a machine language. They are used to store and manipulate information automatically. (11)

PUNCHED PAPER TAPE — See "Punched Cards." (11)

RECORDS — Any paper, book, photograph, microfilm, map, drawing, chart, card, magnetic tape, or similar media, or any copy or printout thereof, that has been created in, or received by, a company in connection with its activities.

RECORDS CENTER — A centralized grouping of records of primary or secondary importance to a company; or a repository for the inactive records of a company. (10)

RECORDS MANAGEMENT — The function of planning, organizing, coordinating, directing, controlling, and supervising all types of records within a corporation or organization from their creation to final disposition.

RELEASE MARKS – A notation or check mark that indicates that a record is ready for filing. (3)

RELATIVE INDEX – A guiding classification of subject aspects physically separate from the file to which it relates. (7)

RELEASE MARKS – A notation or check mark that indicates that a record is ready for filing. (3)

REQUISITION SLIP – A form used to request records from files. (10)

RETENTION PERIOD – The length of time records are considered useful and therefore are to be kept in a company. (10)

RETENTION SCHEDULE – A listing of dates to which records are to be kept. (10) See "Destruction Schedule."

SCORING – An impression across the bottom of a folder that makes it easy to crease it, thus accommodating bulky materials. (5)

SECONDARY GUIDE – Guides that subdivide the primary sections of a file. (4)

SECURITY CENTER – A location where important company records are safely stored. It may be a bomb shelter located outside the city. (10)

SEQUENTIAL (SERIAL) NUMBERING – Consecutive numbering. For example, 1, 3, 5. (7)

SERIAL, CONSECUTIVE, SEQUENCE, ORDERED – Adjectives describing numbering systems where one item follows another in an order without interruption. (7)

SHELF FILING – System that uses open shelves, rather than cabinets, for storing the records. (5)

SIGNALS – Plastic or metal devices that are fastened to papers and folders to get attention. Signals are usually found in card and visible files. (9)

SIGNIFICANT NUMBERS – A number having connotation, an interpretative meaning. For example, license plate 1–69–65 might mean Douglas County, 69,000 issued in 1965. (7)

SIZING – The stiffness that results from the chemical treatment of paper fibers. (5)

SLIDING SIGNALS – Movable devices, generally plastic, on the open edge of a visible card file. (9)

SORTING – Placing, separating, or arranging of items according to class or kind. (3)

SOUNDEX – An indexing system in which all names that sound alike (but are spelled differently) are filed together. (4)

STAGGERED POSITION — An arrangement of folders in which their tabs are in an advancing, progressive sequence; 1st position, 2nd position, etc. (5) See "Position."

STANDARD — A guide established by authority as a criterion or a model. (2)

STANDARDIZED CLASSIFICATIONS — Predetermined arrangements of information. They are established by authority as the best possible arrangements to follow. (4)

STANDARD PRACTICE INSTRUCTION (SPI) or STANDARD OPERATING PROCEDURE (SOP) — A standardized or agreed-on written description of procedure to follow. (10)

STATUTE OF LIMITATIONS — The time limit within which an action may legally be brought upon a contract. (10)

STORING — Putting records in some type of file. (10)

SUBCLASSIFICATIONS — Items within a subordinate phase of a classification scheme. (4) See "Secondary Guides."

SUBJECT FILING — Arranging records alphabetically by names of topics or things, rather than by individual names. (6)

SUBSTITUTION CARD — A card put in a folder to indicate that a record has been borrowed. It tells who has it. (10)

SURNAME — An individual's last or family name. (2)

SYSTEM — A combination of interrelating parts that make up a whole. The identity of the parts depends on the type of system. A filing system, for example, might contain the following parts: equipment, supplies, personnel, standard procedures and methods, files, and machines. (4) See "Systems and Procedures."

SYSTEMS AND PROCEDURES — A procedure is a particular combination of parts within a system; a series of related steps that is within or subordinate to a system.

TAB — The projection on a folder or guide on which the caption is written. Tabs are of various sizes. (5)

TAILOR-MADE SYSTEM — Course of action designed to meet the special needs of a particular business or situation. (4) See "System." Opposite of "Prefabricated System."

TAPE LIBRARIAN — One who maintains a collection of tapes. (11)

TERMINAL-DIGIT FILING — A method of filing by the last digits (usually the last two) of a number instead of by the first digits as in traditional left-to-right reading. (7)

TICKLER FILE — A chronological file that calls attention to due dates for records or items that need action. (10)

TRANSFER — Removing inactive records from the active files. (10)

TRANSFER FILE — A file of relatively inactive material that has been or is to be moved from active files. (10)

UNIT — Each part of a name that is used in indexing. (2)

UNIT RECORDS — Identifiable, standardized items or pieces of information, (9) See "Filing Unit."

UNITIZED MICROFILM — See "Aperture Card," "Chips," and "Card Unit." (11)

VARIABLE INFORMATION — Information that is recorded or collected on a form and that changes from form to form such as an individual's name. (9)

VERTICAL FILING — Storing records on their edges. (9)

VISIBLE FILING — Cards with exposed surfaces so that key data can be seen at a glance. (9)

VITAL RECORDS — Those necessary to the life or continuity of a company. (10)

WORK STATION — The area where an individual works. In an office it is usually composed of a desk, a chair, and possibly a file.

B

Filing Equipment and
Supply Companies

Filing equipment and supply companies represent a major source of information for both traditional and new types of equipment and supplies. Much research is performed by vendors to improve the quality of their products and to develop new systems. Many are regular advertisers in trade journals (including those listed in Appendix D-4) where one can see some of the products illustrated. A simple inquiry usually results in information about models, specifications, and helpful tips on how to manage records more efficiently.

The following is a list of some vendors.

Acco Products, Inc.
5150 N. Northwest Highway
Chicago, Illinois 60630

Acme Visible Records, Inc.
2106 W. Allview Drive
Crozet, Va. 22932

Adapto Steel Products
3770 Northwest 52nd Street
Miami, Fla.

Advance Products, Inc.
76-05 51st Avenue
Elmhurst, L.I., N.Y. 11373

G. J. Aigner Corp.
426 South Clinton St.
Chicago, Illinois 60607

Alden Systems Co.
258 North Main Street
Brockton, Mass.

All-Steel Equipment, Inc.
Box 871
Aurora, Ill.

Amberg File & Index Co.
1627 Duane Blvd.
Kankakee, Ill, 60607

Ames Colorfile Corp.
21 Vine Street
Somerville, Mass. 02143

Anderson-Hickey Co.
Box 8038
Nashville, Tenn.

Art Metal, Inc.
Jones & Gifford Avenue
Jamestown, N.Y.

Art Steel Co.
170 West 233rd Street
Bronx, N.Y.

Bankers Box Co.
2607 North 25th Avenue
Franklin Park, Ill. 60131

Barkley Corp.
1220 W. Van Buren Street
Chicago, Ill. 60607

Bernard-Franklin Co., Inc.
4045 Torresdale Avenue
Philadelphia, Pa.

Boorum & Pease Co.
84 Hudson Avenue
Brooklyn, New York

Brown-Morse Co.
110 East Broadway
Muskegon, Mich.

Buddy Products, Inc.
1318 South Leavitt Street
Chicago, Ill.

Burroughs Division
Lear Siegler, Inc.
3000 North Burdick Street
Kalamazoo, Mich.

Business Efficiency Aids, Inc.
8114 N. Lawndale Avenue
Skokie, Ill. 60076

Business & Indeustrial Furniture, Inc.
611 North Broadway
Milwaukee, Wis.

Cel-U-Del Corp.
23 McArther Ave.
New Windsor, N.Y. 12550

Challenger Steel Products Corp.
350 Morgan Avenue
Brooklyn, N.Y.

Cole Steel Equipment Co., Inc.
Division Litton Industries
415 Madison Avenue
New York, N.Y.

Columbia Hallowell
Hatfield, Pennsylvannia 19440

Columbia Office Furniture
Division Standard Pressed Steel
Co.
Hatfield, Pa.

Consolidated Business Products
1318 S. Leavitt Street
Chicago, Ill. 60608

Convoy, Inc.
P.O. Box G, Station B
Canton, Ohio

Corry Jamestown Corp.
840 East Columbus Avenue
Curry, Pa.

Diebold, Inc.
2011 Mulberry Rd.
Canton, Ohio 44703

Dolin Metal Products, Inc.
315 Lexington Avenue
Brooklyn, N.Y. 11216

Eck-Adams Corp.
Box 103
Peru, Ind.

V. W. Eimicke Associates, Inc.
P. O. Box 160
Bronxville, New York 10708

Elbe File & Binder Corp.
649 Alden Street
Fall River, Mass. 02723

Equipto
225 South Highland
Aurora, Ill.

Fidelity File Box, Inc.
705 Pennsylvannia Avenue South
Minneapolis, Minn.

Fortress, Inc.
15531 East Arrow Highway
Irvindale, Calif.

Frontier Manufacturing Co.
11200 Hines Boulevard
Dallas, Texas

General Binding Co.
1101 Skokie Highway
Northbrook, Ill. 60062

General Fireproofing Co.
East Dennick Avenue
Youngstown, Ohio

Gillotte, R. P. Co., Inc.
929 Holland Avenue
Cayce, S.C. 29003

Globe-Wernicke Co.
1505 Jefferson
Toledo, Ohio 43624

Hamilton Cosco, Inc.
Box 200
Gallatin, Tenn.

Harrison Steel Desk & File Co.
4718 West Fifth Avenue
Chicago, Ill.

Haskell of Pittsburgh
Box 5273
Pittsburgh, Pa.

Hedges Manufacturing Co.
P.O. Box 92
1441 Circle Avenue
Forest Park, Ill.

High Point Furniture, Inds.
High Point, N.C.

Horizon Steel Products, Inc.
223 Water Street
Brooklyn, N.Y.

Inca Metal Products Corp.
Box 398
Carrollton, Texas

Invincible Metal Furniture Co.
26th & Franklin Street
Manitowoc, Wis.

Jeffco Industries, Inc.
76 4th Street
Somerville, N.J. 08876

Jefsteel Business Equipment
  Corp.
1345 Halsey Street
Brooklyn, N.Y.

Kwik-File, Inc.
2845 Harriet Avenue South
Minneapolis, Minn.

LeFebure Corp.
308 29th Street N.E.
Cedar Rapids, Iowa

Lit-Ning Products Co.
7001 North Clark
Chicago, Ill.

Litton Automated Bus. Systems
600 Washington Avenue
Carlstadt, N.J. 07072

Luckett Loose Leaf, Ltd.
44 Atomic Avenue
Toronto, Ontario, Canada

Lyon Metal Products, Inc.
78 Railroad Avenue
Aurora, Ill.

Marnay Sales & Mfg. Co., Inc.
41 East 42nd Street
New York, New York 10017

Metalstand Co.
11200 Roosevelt Boulevard
Philadelphia, Pa.

Modern Steelcraft Co.
1101 Linwood Street
Brooklyn, N.Y.

Mosler Co.
1561 Grand Blvd.
Hamilton, Ohio 45012

National Blank Book Co.
P. O. Box 791
Holyoke, Mass. 01042

Northwest Metal Products Co.
1337 East Mason Street
Green Bay, Wisc.

Oxford Filing Supply Co., Inc.
Clinton Road
Garden City, N.Y. 11530

Paige Co., Inc.
432 Park Avenue South
New York, New York 10016

Parker Steel Products, Inc.
54 North 11th Street
Brooklyn, N.Y.

Peerless Steel Equipment Co.
6600 Hasbrook Avenue
Philadelphia, Pa.

Plan Hold Corp.
P. O. Box 3458
Torrance, Ca. 90510

Remington Rand Office Systems
P. O. Box 171
Marietta, Ohio 45750

Shaw-Walker Co.
1950 Townsend St.
Muskegon, Mich. 49443

Shelves, Unlimited
1134 First Avenue
New York, N.Y.

Smead Mfg. Co.
309-311 Second Street
Hastings, Minn. 55033

Solid Industries, Inc.
221 West 17th Street
New York, N.Y.

Steel Fixtures Manufacturing Co.
Box 917
Topeka, Kansas

Steel Parts Manufacturing Co.
4630 West Harrison Street
Chicago, Ill.

Steelcase, Inc.
1120 East 36th Street
Grand Rapids, Mich. 49501

Straube Inds., Inc.
One Palmer Square
Princeton, N.J.

Supreme Equipment & Systems
   Corp.
170 53rd Street
Brooklyn, N.Y. 11232

Tab Products Co.
2690 Hannover St.
Box 10269
Palo Alto, Calif. 94304

Tennsco Corporation
Box 326
Dickson, Tenn.

S. E. & M. Vernon, Inc.
801 Newark Avenue
Elizabeth, N.J. 07208

Vertiflex Co.
630 West 41st Street
Chicago, Ill.

Victor Systems & Equipment
107 Putnam Street
Marietta, Ohio

Visirecord, Inc.
54 Railroad Avenue
Copaigue, L.I., N.Y. 11726

Warshaw Mfg. Co.
4000 First Avenue
Brooklyn, N.Y. 11232

Wassell Organization, Inc.
25 Syvan Road South
Box 390
Westport, Conn. 06880

Watson Manufacturing Co.
63 Taylor Street
Jamestown, N.Y.

Western Manufacturing Co.
546 North Highland Avenue
Aurora, Ill.

Wheeldex & Simila Products,
   Inc.
1000 North Division Street
Peekskill, N.Y. 10566

Williams Office Furniture Co.
One Park Avenue
New York, N.Y.

Wilson-Jones Co.
6150 Touhy Avenue
Chicago, Ill. 60648

C

Filing and Records
Management Associations

A representative list of national and international associations in which filing experts might be interested is provided below. A number of new associations have been formed in the past two decades. Some have limited relationships to filing and records management but are still worth considering for information and for becoming a member.

The values in joining a technical association vary for different participants, usually depending upon one's job. Most associations have regular monthly meetings with speakers, hold periodic conferences, and publish journals and/or reference materials. Although speakers afford an exposure to new ideas, the opportunity to meet and exchange information with other members is probably even more valuable. Check an association carefully before joining to ensure that it will serve your needs.

Administrative Management Society
Willow Grove, Pa. 19090

American Medical Record Association
875 N. Michigan Avenue–Suite 1850
Chicago, Ill. 60611

American Library Association
50 East Huron Street
Chicago, Ill. 60611

American Management Association
135 West 50th Street
New York, N.Y. 10020

American Records Management Association
24 North Wabash Avenue, Suite 823
Chicago, Ill. 60602

Association for Systems Management
24587 Bagley Road
Cleveland, Ohio 44138

Business Forms Management Association
P. O. Box 54192, Terminal Annex
Los Angeles, Calif. 90054

Data Processing Management Association
404 North Wesley Avenue
Mount Morris, Ill. 61054

National Business Forms Association
1522 "K" Street N.W.
Washington, D.C. 20005

National Fire Protection Association
60 Batterymarch Street
Boston, Mass. 02110

National Microfilm Association
250 Prince George Street
Annapolis, Md. 21401

National Secretaries Association
1103 Grand Avenue
Kansas City, Mo. 64106

Society of American Archivists
3110 Elm Avenue
Baltimore, Md. 21211

Society of Reproduction Engineers
18307 James Couzens
Detroit, Mich. 48235

Special Libraries Association
31 East 10th Street
New York, N.Y. 10003

D

A Filing and
Records Management Bibliography

A growing recognition of the problems associated with maintaining records has resulted in an increase in publications on the subject. Available are magazines, books, handbooks, and leaflets documented by industry; by federal, state, and local levels of government; and by vendors of records and information systems equipment. A popular source of information is current articles featured in the periodicals. (See List of Periodicals, Appendix D–4.)

The following is a representative list of books, handbooks, manuals, and articles.

1. Books

Bassett, E. D., Peter L. Agnew, and Daniel Goodman. *Business Filing and Records Control*. Cincinnati: South-Western Publishing Company, 1964.

Becker, Joseph and Robert M. Hayes. *Information Storage and Retrieval*: Tools, Elements, Theories. New York: John Wiley & Sons, Inc., 1963.

Benedon, William. *Records Management*. Englewood Cliffs, N.J.: Prentice-Hall, Inc., 1968.

Blegen, August L. *Records Management Step-by-Step*. Stamford, Conn.: Office Publications, Inc., 1965.

Bourne, Charles P. *Methods of Information Handling*. New York: John Wiley & Sons, Inc., 1963.

Case Studies in Records Retention and Control. New York: The Controllership Foundation (now Financial Executives Research Foundation), 1957.

Clark, Jesse L. *Records Management.* Newton, Mass.: Paperwork Systems, 1970.

Collison, Robert L. *Modern Business Filing and Archives.* London: Ernest Benn Limited (order from John De Graff, Inc., N.Y.), 1963.

Dickinson, A. Litchard. *Filing and Finding in the Office.* Elmhurst, Ill.: The Business Press, 1964.

Fahrner, William F., and W. E. Gibbs. *Basic Rules of Alphabetic Filing* (Programmed Instruction). Cincinnati: South-Western Publishing Company, 1965.

Griffin, Mary Claire. *Records Management: A Modern Tool for Business.* Boston: Allyn and Bacon, Inc., 1964.

Johnson, Mina M., and Norman F. Kallaus. *Records Management.* Cincinnati: South-Western Publishing Company, 1967.

Kahn, Gilbert, Theodore Kahn, and Jeffrey R. Stewart, Jr. *Progressive Filing and Records Management.* New York: Gregg Publishing Division, McGraw-Hill Book Company, 1962.

Kish, Joseph L., Jr., and James Morris. *Microfilm in Business.* New York: Ronald Press, 1966.

Leahy, Emmet J., and Christopher A. Cameron. *Modern Records Management.* New York: McGraw-Hill Book Company, 1965.

Littlefield, C. L., and R. L. Peterson. *Modern Office Management.* Englewood Cliffs, N.J.: Prentice-Hall, Inc., 1964.

Place, Irene, Charles Hicks, and Robin Wilkinson. *Office Management.* Boston: Allyn and Bacon, Inc., 1971.

Place, Irene and Estelle Popham. *Filing and Records Management* (and Teachers Key). Englewood Cliffs, N.J.: Prentice-Hall, Inc., 1966.

Rademaker, T., ed. *Business Systems,* Volume II. Cleveland: Systems and Procedures Association, 1963.

Ross, H. John. *Paperwork Management.* South Miami: Office Research Institute, 1962.

Schellenberg, T. R. *The Management of Archives.* New York: Columbia University Press, 1965.

_____ . *Modern Archives, Principles and Techniques.* Chicago: The University of Chicago Press, 1964.

_____ . *Office Management and Control.* Homewood, Ill.: Richard D. Irwin, Inc., 1965.

Selden, William H., *et al. Filing and Finding.* Englewood Cliffs, N.J.: Prentice-Hall, Inc., 1962.

Terry, George R. *Office Systems and Procedures.* Homewood, Ill.: Dow Jones-Irwin, Inc., 1966.

Weeks, Bertha M. *Filing and Records Management.* New York: Ronald Press, 1964.

Weld, Christopher M. *Office Manager's Handbook.* Chicago: Dartnell Corporation, 1958.

Wylie, Harry, ed. *Office Management Handbook.* New York: Ronald Press, 1959.

2. Handbooks and Manuals

Blanchard, Marvin L. *Records Disposition.* Dept. of Finance, State of California, 1961.

Chamberlin, Coleman R. *Filing Facts.* National Filing Aid Bureau, 342 Madison Avenue, New York, N.Y., 1963.

College and University Retention and Disposition Schedule. State Dept. of Archives and History, Raleigh, N.C., 1964.

Cutting Costs with Records Management. American Telephone and Telegraph Co., 1957.

Federal Agencies: Federal Government Printing Office, Washington, D.C.

Applying Retention Schedules. 1961.

Bibliography for Records Managers. 1965.

Checklist for Appraising Files Operation in Your Office. 1968.

The Federal Paperwork Jungle. House Report No. 52, 89th Congress, 1st sess., 1965.

Federal Records Centers. 1967.

File Stations. 1967.

Files Maintenance & Disposition. Dept. of Defense, February, 1968.

Files Operations. 1964.

Guide to Records Retention Requirements. Updated Annually.

List of National Archives Microfilm Publications. 1966.

Protecting Vital Records. 1958.

Protection of Vital Records. July 1966.

Subject Filing. 1966.

Filing Equipment Comparisons and Costs. Filing Equipment Sales Division of the General Fireproofing Co., Youngstown, Ohio, 1953.

Guide for the Retention and Preservation of Records. Records Controls, Inc., and American Assoc. of Hospital Accountants, 1967.

Guide to Selected Readings in Records Management. National Records Management Council, Inc., 50 E. 42nd St., New York, N.Y., 1954.

Lucas, Joseph W. *More Profit – Less Paper.* Standard Oil Co. of California, 1953.

Mitchell, William E. *Records Retention – A Practical Guide.* Ellsworth Publishing Co., 314 Newcastle Road, Syracuse, N.Y., 1959.

Payne, Marjorie Thomas. *File This, Please!* Dartnell Corporation, 4460 Ravenswood Avenue, Chicago, Illinois 60640, 1967.

Protection of Records. National Fire Protection Assoc., 60 Batterymarch St., Boston, Mass., 1967.

Records Control and Storage Handbook. Bankers Box Co., Franklin Park, Ill., 1965.

Reference Manual Form and Card Design. Data Processing Div., International Business Machines Corp., East Post Road, White Plains, N.Y., 1962.

Retention of Records. American Assoc. of Collegiate Registrars and Admissions Officers, 1960.

3. Articles

"A Case Study: Retention Scheduling at the University of Washington," Harry N. Fujita. *Records Management Quarterly,* October 1968.

"Administrative Problems of Records Management," Freida Kraines. *The Office,* September 1965.

"Automated Records Keeping," Daniel Peck. *Administrative Management,* April 1966.

"Mail Management," Terry Beach. *Records Management Journal,* Summer 1969.

"People and Records," Irene Place. *Records Management Quarterly,* July 1967.

"Records Storage Cost Analysis," John Fellowes. *Systems,* May 1966.

"Rush Retrieval With Mechanized Files." *Modern Office Procedures,* February 1970.

"Teaching IRM in College," E. Mark Langemo and William M. Mitchell. *Information and Records Management.* February-March 1970.

"The Status of Business Archives," Robert W. Lovett. *The American Archivist,* July 1969.

"What Can COM Do For Us?" J. R. Antal. *Datamation,* December 1969.

"What's Ahead in Manual Filing," *Modern Office Procedures,* September 1970.

4. Periodicals

The periodicals listed below are representative of those which contain articles on filing and records management. This list does not include publications of vendors, many of which are well worth exploring.

Only a few periodicals give full attention to filing and records management, but most office magazines contain occasional articles that specifically apply to one or more of the filing activities. Articles are valuable as supplementary reading to workbooks, particularly for information on the latest technological developments. Case studies often describe specific applications.

Most articles are indexed in the *Readers' Guide to Periodical Literature* or the *Social Sciences and Humanities Index.* However, some of the new periodicals will not yet be included. In such cases, check either the magazine's accumulative indexes or the tables of contents of each issue.

A representative list of articles published in these periodicals is noted in Section 3 of Appendix D.

Title	Address	Periodicity
Administrative Management	Geyer-McAllister Publications 51 Madison Avenue New York, New York 10010	Monthly
American Archivist, The	Monumental Printing Co. 3110 Elm Avenue Baltimore, Md. 21211	Quarterly
Business Automation	Business Press International, Inc. 288 Park Avenue West Elmhurst, Ill. 60126	Monthly
Business Graphics	Graphic Arts Publishing Company 7373 No. Lincoln Avenue Chicago, Illinois 60646	Monthly
Computer Decisions	Hayden Publications Co., Inc. 850 Third Avenue New York, N.Y. 10022	Monthly

Title	*Address*	*Periodicity*
Computers and Automation	Berkeley Enterprises, Inc. 815 Washington Street Newtonville, Mass. 02160	Monthly
Datamation	F. D. Thompson Publications, Inc. 35 Mason Street Greenwich, Conn. 06830	Monthly
EDP Analyzer	Canning Publications, Inc. 134 Escondido Avenue Vista, Calif. 92083	Monthly
Industrial Engineering	American Institute of Industrial Engineering 345 East 47th Street New York, N.Y. 10017	Monthly
Information and Records Management	Information and Records Management, Inc. 41 East 28th Street New York, N.Y. 10016	Bimonthly
Journal of Data Management	Data Management Association 505 Busse Highway Park Ridge, Ill. 60068	Monthly
Journal of Educational Data Processing	Educational Systems Corporation P. O. Box 2995 Stanford, Calif. 94305	Quarterly
Journal of Systems Management	Association for Systems Management 2487 Bagley Road Cleveland, Ohio 44138	Monthly
Modern Office Procedures	Modern Office Procedures Magazine P. O. Box 5746-U Cleveland, Ohio 44115	Monthly
The Office	Office Publications, Inc. 73 Southfield Avenue Stamford, Conn. 06904	Monthly
Office Products News	United Technical Publications, Inc. 645 Stewart Avenue Garden City, N.Y. 11530	Nine times each year
Prologue: The Journal of The National Archives	Prologue: The Journal of The National Archives National Archives Building Washington, D.C. 20408	Quarterly
Records Management Journal	Association of Records Executives and Administrators P. O. Box 4259 Grand Central Station New York, N.Y. 10017	Quarterly

Title	Address	Periodicity
Records Management Quarterly	American Records Management Association 24 North Wabash Avenue, Suite 823 Chicago, Ill. 60602	Quarterly
Reproductions Review	North American Publishing Co. 134 North 13th St. Philadelphia, Pa. 19107	Quarterly
Systems	United Business Publications, Inc. 200 Madison Avenue New York, N.Y. 10016	Monthly

E

Standard Divisions for Alphabetic Guides

60 Divisions

A	Cr	H	Li	Pe	St
Am	D	He	M	Pi	Su
B	De	Ho	Mar	Q	T
Be	Do	Hu	Mc	R	To
Bi	E	I	Me	Ri	U
Br	F	J	Mo	Ro	V
Bu	Fi	K	Mu	S	W
C	G	Ki	N	Sch	We
Ch	Gi	L	O	Se	Wi
Co	Gr	Le	P	Si	XYZ

100 Divisions

A	Cl	Fr	John	Ni	Sp
Al	Co	G	K	O	St
Am	Con	Ge	Ke	P	Sto
Ander	Cor	Go	Ki	Pe	T
Ar	Cr	Gr	Kn	Pi	Tho
B	Cu	Gro	L	Pr	Ti
Bar	D	H	Le	Q-R	Tr
Be	De	Ham	Li	Ri	U
Ber	Di	Har	Lo	Ro	V
Bi	Do	Hat	M	Ros	W
Bo	Dow	He	Man	S	War
Br	E	Hi	McA	Sch	We
Bro	El	Ho	Me	Se	Wh
Bu	Et	Hon	Mi	Sh	Wi
C	F	Hu	Mo	Si	Wo
Car	Fi	I	Mu	Smith	XYZ
Ch	Fo	J	N		

150 Divisions

A	Co	Gar	Jones	Mu	Sp
Al	Con	Ge	K	N	St
Am	Coo	Gi	Ke	Ni	Sto
Ander	Cor	Go	Kel	O	Su
Ar	Cr	Gr	Ki	Or	T
At	Cu	Gre	Kn	P	Te
B	D	Gro	Kr	Pe	Tho
Baker	Davis	H	L	Pet	Ti
Bar	De	Hal	Lar	Pi	Tr
Be	Del	Ham	Le	Pr	U
Ber	Di	Har	Lei	Pu	V
Bi	Do	Harr	Li	Q-R	Ve
Bl	Dow	Hat	Lo	Re	W
Bo	Du	He	Lu	Ri	Wall
Bon	E	Hen	M	Ro	War
Br	El	Her	Man	Ros	We
Bro	Et	Hi	Mas	Ru	Wei
Bu	F	Ho	McA	S	Wh
Bur	Fe	Hol	McD	Sch	Wi
C	Fi	Hon	McK	Schm	Williams
Car	Fl	Hu	Me	Se	Wilson
Cas	Fo	Hun	Mi	Sh	Wo
Ch	Fr	I	Miller	Si	Wr
Che	Fri	J	Mo	Smith	XY
Cl	G	John	Mor	Sn	Z

200 Divisions

A	Con	Green	Lar	Or	Sn
Ad	Coo	Gri	Le	P	Sp
Adams	Cor	Gu	Li	Par	St
Al	Cr	H	Lo	Pat	Stone
Allen	Cu	Ham	Lor	Pe	Str
Am	D	Har	Lu	Per	Su
American	Davis	Harr	M	Ph	Sw
Ar	De	Has	Mah	Pi	T
As	Dem	He	Man	Po	Th
B	Di	Hen	Mar	Pr	Ti
Bal	Do	Her	Mart	Pu	To
Bar	Dor	Hi	Mas	Q	Tr
Bas	Dr	Ho	Mc	R	Tu
Be	Du	Hom	McD	Re	U
Ben	E	Hos	McI	Ri	United
Bi	Ed	Hu	McM	Rid	V
Bl	El	Hun	Me	Roc	Ve
Bo	En	I	Mer	Ros	Vo
Br	Es	J	Mi	Ross	W

Bre	F	Je	Miller	Ru	Wal
Bro	Fe	Jo	Min	S	War
Brown	Federal	John	Mo	San	We
Bu	Fi	Jon	Mor	Sc	Wel
Bur	Fl	Jones	Mos	Sch	Wes
C	Fo	K	Mu	Schu	White
Cam	Fr	Ke	Mur	Se	Wi
Car	Fri	Kem	N	Sh	Wil
Cas	G	Ki	National	Sher	Wils
Ch	Ge	Ko	Ne	Si	Wo
Che	Gi	Kr	Ni	Sim	Wr
Ci	Gl	Ku	No	Sk	X
Cl	Go	L	O	Sm	Y
Co	Gold	Lan	Ol	Smith	Z
Collins	Gr				

F

Retention Schedule

Diebold* includes in a management study the following recommendations for length of time to keep important company records:

ACCOUNTING, AUDITING, EXECUTIVE, AND ADMINISTRATIVE DEPT.

Type of Record	Recommended Retention Period
Accounts Receivable	7 Years
Accounts Payable	7 Years
Annual Reports	Permanent
Appraisals	Permanent
Assets and Property Records	Permanent
Audit Reports	Permanent
Authorization & Appropriations for Expenditure	Permanent
Bank Statements and Reconciliation	Permanent
Bond and Bondholders' Records	Permanent
Bonds, Surety	3 Yrs. after Expiration
Building Plans and Specifications	Permanent
Cancelled Stock Certificates	Optional
Capital Stock Certificates	Permanent
Capital Stock Ledgers	Permanent
Certificates of Incorporation	Permanent
Charge Sales Slips	7 Years
Charter	Permanent
Check Books	Permanent

*Diebold, Inc., 2011 Mulberry Road, Canton, Ohio 44703.

233

Type of Record	Recommended Retention Period
Checks, Cancelled and Stop Payment Notices	Permanent
Claim Files	Permanent
Consolidated Balance Sheets	Permanent
Constitution and By-Laws	Permanent
Consular Invoices	7 Years
Contracts and Agreements	Permanent
Contracts, War	4 Yrs. after Duration
Control Ledgers	Permanent
Corporate Records	Permanent
Correspondence, Executive	Permanent
Correspondence, General	7 Years
Cost Sheets	Permanent
Credit Tickets	7 Years
Deeds	Permanent
Departmental Reports	7 Years
Deposit Books and Slips	7 Years
Destruction Records	Permanent
Dividend Checks	Permanent
Drafts Paid	Permanent
Easements	Permanent
Fidelity Bonds	3 Yrs. after Expiration
Financial Statements	Permanent
Franchises	Permanent
General Books of Account	Permanent
Journals	
Cash Disbursed	
Cash Received	
General	
Miscellaneous	
Purchase	
Sales	
Ledgers	
Accounts Payable	
Accounts Receivable	
Exchange	
Expense	
General	
Merchandise	
Miscellaneous	
Notes Payable	
Notes Receivable	
Property and Equipment Subsidiary	
General Code and Cipher Books	Permanent
House Organs	Permanent
Insurance Policies	7 Yrs. after Expiration
Insurance Schedules	7 Yrs. after Expiration
Inventory Records	Permanent
Investment Records	Permanent
Leases	Permanent
Letter of Credit	Permanent

| | *Recommended Retention Period* |
Type of Record	
Licenses	Permanent
Manifests	7 Years
Minutes of Meetings	Permanent
Miscellaneous Reports	7 Years
Mortgages	Permanent
Notes, Cancelled	7 Years
Notes Receivable	7 Years
Options	Until Expiration
Petty Cash Records	2 Years
Priority Records	7 Years
Property Records	Permanent
Proxies	2 Years
Real Estate Acquisitions	Permanent
Requisition on Stores or for Purchases	3 Years
Research Data	Permanent
Retired Securities	Optional
Royalty Records	Permanent
Safe Deposit Vault Records	Permanent
Signatures	Permanent
Statistical Reports	Permanent
Stock and Stockholders' Records	Permanent
Stock Transfer Records	Permanent
Stop Payment Orders	Permanent
Tabulating Cards	7 Years
Tax Records	Permanent
Trial Balances	Permanent
Vouchers	7 Years
War Contracts	Optional
Water Rights	Permanent

ADVERTISING DEPARTMENT

| | *Recommended Retention Period* |
Type of Record	
Contracts with Agencies, Engravers, Lithographers and Printers	7 Years
Correspondence, Executive	Permanent
Correspondence, General	7 Years
Department Form Proofs	Optional
Dummies and Layouts	Optional
Inquiries Record	Optional
Inventory of Advertising Material	Optional
Mailings Record	7 Years
Manuscripts	Optional
Market Investigations	Permanent
Newspaper Clippings	Optional
Orders for Advertising	7 Years

Type of Record	Recommended Retention Period
Photographs and Photostats	Optional
Production, Progress and Job Records	7 Years
Publication File	Permanent
Requisitions for Advertising	7 Years
Sketches	Optional
Testimonial Letters	Optional

COST DEPARTMENT

Type of Record	Recommended Retention Period
Cost Production and Job Summary Records	Permanent
Labor Distribution Records	7 Years
Time and Earning Records	7 Years

CREDIT AND COLLECTION DEPARTMENT

Type of Record	Recommended Retention Period
Application for Credit	7 Years
Collection Files	7 Years
Credit Authorization Records	7 Years
Credit Files — Commercial Reports	7 Years
Financial Statements, Letters of Reference, etc.	
Time Payment Contracts and Promissory Notes	7 Years

ENGINEERING AND PRODUCTION DEPARTMENT

Type of Record	Recommended Retention Period
Uncollectible Accounts	7 Years
Analysis and Compound Records	Permanent
Blueprints, Drawings, Sketches, Tracings, Index Cards, Charts and Graphs	Permanent
Die and Tool Records	Permanent
Experiment and Test Records	Permanent
Flow of Work and Material Charts	Permanent
Formulas	Permanent
Laboratory Production Records	Permanent
Machine and Product Production Records	Permanent
Maps	Permanent
Operating Reports	Permanent
Order Procedures	Permanent

Type of Record	Recommended Retention Period
Patterns	Permanent
Planning Summaries	Permanent
Plant Inventory and Machine Location Records	Permanent
Plant Layout Charts	Permanent
Production, Progress and Job Records	Permanent
Research Data File	Permanent
Specification Sheets	Permanent
Templates	Permanent
Time Cards and Reports	Permanent
Work or Shop Orders	Permanent

ESTIMATING AND PRICING

Type of Record	Recommended Retention Period
Correspondence	7 Years
Estimates	7 Years
Price Records	7 Years
Quotations	7 Years
Specifications	7 Years

LEGAL DEPARTMENT

Type of Record	Recommended Retention Period
Case Files, Affidavits, Testimony, Depositions, etc.	Permanent
Claims, Evidences and Proofs	Permanent
Copyrights and Applications for Dockets	Permanent
Information File, Briefs, etc.	Permanent
Patents and Applications for Tax Files, Returns, Briefs, Appeals	Permanent
Trade Mark and Applications for Titles and Mortgages, Deeds	Permanent

MAILING DEPARTMENT

Type of Record	Recommended Retention Period
Parcel Post Insurance Receipts	3 Years
Registered Letter Receipts	3 Years

238

ORDER DEPARTMENT

Type of Record	Recommended Retention Period
Acknowledgments of Orders	3 Years
Inspection Records	3 Years
Notices of Orders Billed	3 Years
Order, Register	3 Years
Order Replacement Record	3 Years
Orders, Filled	3 Years
Orders, Unfilled	3 Years
Returned Goods Record	3 Years
Shipping Notices and Reports	3 Years

ORGANIZATION STUDIES

Type of Record	Recommended Retention Period
Any Evidence of Payment for Service	Permanent
Discharge Tickets	Permanent
Payroll Receipts	Permanent
Payroll Records	Permanent
Pension Plan Records	Permanent
Personnel Records	7 Years
Receipted Pay Checks	Permanent
Receipted Time Tickets	Permanent
Reference Letters	7 Years
Retirement Records	Permanent
Social Security Records	Permanent
State Wage Reports	Permanent
Time-and-Motion Studies	7 Years
Time Records	7 Years
Unclaimed Wage Record	7 Years
Unemployment Insurance Reports	Permanent
War Bond Delivery Receipts	Permanent
War Bond Pledges	Optional
Workmen's Compensation Reports	Permanent

PERSONNEL DEPARTMENT

Type of Record	Recommended Retention Period
Accident Records	Permanent
Assignment and Garnishee Records	3 Years
Employee Case Histories	7 Years
Employee Contracts	7 Years
Employee Savings Fund Records	Permanent
Employment Releases	7 Years
Federal Wage Records	Permanent

Fingerprint Records	7 Years
Group Insurance Records	Permanent
Hospital Plan Records	7 Years
Invention Assignment Forms	Permanent
Minors' Salary Releases	Optional
War Bond Delivery Receipts	Permanent
War Bond Pledges	Optional
Workmen's Compensation Reports	Permanent
Receipted Pay Checks	Permanent
Receipted Time Tickets	Permanent
Discharge Tickets	Permanent
Any Evidence of Payment for Service	Permanent

PURCHASING DEPARTMENT

Type of Record	*Recommended Retention Period*
Acknowledgments of Orders	3 Years
Contracts with Suppliers	Permanent
Correspondence	3 Years
Invoices	Permanent
Price List Files	Permanent
Printed Forms Inventory	3 Years
Priority Requisitions	3 Years
Purchase and Cost Records	3 Years
Purchase Orders, Filled and Unfilled	3 Years
Quotations	3 Years
Requisitions, Purchase	3 Years
Source of Supply and Catalog Files	3 Years
Specifications	3 Years
Summary of Purchases	3 Years
Vendors' Records	3 Years

SALES DEPARTMENT

Type of Record	*Recommended Retention Period*
Applications for Sales	Optional
Employment Bulletins	Optional
Charts and Graphs	7 Years
Closed Accounts	2 Years
Confidential Contracts	Permanent
Contracts with Customers	7 Years
Contracts with Representatives, Agents, Distributors, etc.	Permanent
Correspondence	7 Years
Correspondence	7 Years
Expense Accounts	7 Years
Filled Contracts	7 Years
Mailing Lists	7 Years

Type of Record	Recommended Retention Period
Market Investigations and Reports	7 Years
Post-War Plans	7 Years
Prospect Records	7 Years
Sales Records and Summaries	7 Years
Sales Territory Layouts, Maps, etc.	7 Years
Salesmen's Reports	7 Years
Special Orders	7 Years
Turnover Comparisons	7 Years
Users' Records	7 Years

SERVICE DEPARTMENT

Type of Record	Recommended Retention Period
Complaints and Service Record	3 Years
Correspondence	3 Years
Returned Goods and Replacements Record	3 Years

STORES DEPARTMENT

Type of Record	Recommended Retention Period
Receiving Reports	3 Years
Requisitions	3 Years
Stock Record	Permanent
Tool Record	3 Years

TRAFFIC DEPARTMENT

Type of Record	Recommended Retention Period
Bills of Lading — Straight and Order	Optional
Claims	7 Years
Correspondence	7 Years
Delivery Receipts	3 Years
Export Declarations	3 Years
Express Receipts	3 Years
Freight Bills	3 Years
Inspection Reports	3 Years
Packing Lists	3 Years
Rate Records	3 Years
Receiving Reports	3 Years
Routing Records	3 Years
Shipping Instructions	3 Years
Shipping Reports	3 Years
Weigh Bills	3 Years

Index